Bingham

Notes

This publication contains the findings from the research of the author and those that provided assistance. It contains several opinions and ideas from the author while trying to explain the credit scoring system. It's intent is to provide an understanding of the system that is both informative and helpful to the reader. The information supplied is of good nature. Any legal advise should be regarded as general information. It is strongly recommended that one contact an attorney or service professional for counsel regarding specific circumstances.

C.P. Publishing

PO Box 1396
Layton, UT 84041-1396

Cover Design by Jordan Jones

Contents

Al Bingham
The Road to 850
Author

Al Bingham has worked in the mortgage industry over the last 15 years. During the last six years, his in-depth research and expertise has been recognized on a state and national level. He has worked extensively on several mortgage related issues. He has given several presentations to elected representatives from across the country to help them understand real estate and mortgage fraud.

Al sits on the State of Utah's education committee that reports to the mortgage commission. He has been a major part in writing two major licensing exams for the mortgage industry within the state of Utah. It is from this experience that Al discovered a lack of understanding of credit and credit scores by a majority in the mortgage industry. He has spent thousands of hours from research and counseling individuals on improving their credit scores. He has developed many strategies over the years to help improve credit scores.

He has created two presentations *Credit Score Plus* and *The Road to 850,* as a supplement to his book. Al is currently working on several other projects to help people improve their credit scores. It is his goal to have people help themselves by identifying means to improve their credit scores.

His information is enlightening and truly refreshing. He has been well received by many organizations both nationally and locally including the *United Way*, the *Utah State Legislature*, and the *Utah Public Employee's Association*.

Al and his wife, Deborah, have four children; Brooklyn, Mackenzie, Andrew, and Aubrey.

Special Thanks & Dedication

Special thanks to all those who have contributed time, research, and experience to this publication including Diane, Brian, Dexter, Debbie, Scott, and Corry Sue. Thanks also goes to my wife, Deborah, for her never ending patience, and to some great parents, Don and Myrle, who taught me so much.

Editors Note

The actual events as outlined this book are true. The names of those involved have been changed so as not to reveal their identity.

Introduction

The 123 point drop in Brian's credit score was unexpected. He and his wife had just purchased their first home a year earlier. All they wanted was a home equity loan to finish the basement as they had two small children and needed more room in the house. They were totally unaware of the future effects on their credit scores and the subsequent financial challenges they would face as they finished their basement.

Brian, who was the sole wage earner, had a credit score of 628 when they initially applied for a home equity loan at a local bank. The bank approved them for a $20,000 at a 7.00% interest rate. They wanted $30,000 to finish the entire basement and decided to look elsewhere.

Even though the interest rate was 18.99%, they elected to take out a $30,000 home equity loan with a finance company. When they tried to refinance the home equity loan to a lower rate with a bank three months later, Brian's credit score had dropped to 505. No lender with a reasonable interest rate would now give them consideration. The couple was stuck, for the foreseeable future, with high monthly payments.

Even though no late payments had been made, Brian's credit score had dropped due to the added credit risks from the type of loan, the type of lender, as well as opening a new account. The score's dramatic drop was primarily the result of adding several credit risks together at the same time.

They would eventually fall behind on mortgage monthly payments and come close to losing their home. If they only had known the factors that drive credit scores, they could have avoided making a poor decision. They were stuck with the consequences, and had few solutions to resolve the problem.

Similar stories, though less dramatic, play out everyday across America. Over the last decade, credit scores have rapidly become a very personal and influential three digit number. These scores are intended to determine our level of risk to financial institutions. We all have some semblance of risk. The question is, *"How much risk?"*

Since the major credit bureaus have released limited information on the makeup of credit scores, many consumers have little understanding or direction. A great deal of misinformation is currently circulated among the general public. As a consequence, we often fail to understand or recognize those important factors that influence credit scores.

This book is designed to help us identify those issues that can impact our credit scores. The proven strategies provide a road map to assist us along our way. By understanding each risk factor and developing strategies, we can make better decisions that make it easier to increase our credit scores.

With higher credit scores, we can save hundreds and even thousands of dollars on insurance premiums and on interest charges annually. Since more employers are requesting credit scores from job applicants, greater employment opportunities with higher compensation may be available. Having an 800 credit score is vital for creating additional financial opportunities.

1

The Cost of a Credit Score

When was the first time you heard of a credit score? The answers range from yesterday to 100 years ago. In many instances, we were probably unaware of the impact of credit scores until we recently applied for a mortgage, auto, or other type of consumer loan. Credit scores have officially been around since 1995. However, they have only been widely used in the last few years for financial and employment purposes.

Having low credit scores can now cost us not only with higher interest rates, they can also cost us from higher insurance premiums and fewer employment possibilities. The extent of our credit score's influence is rapidly increasing to many areas of our financial interest.

The Purpose

What is the purpose of a credit score? Recent surveys have demonstrated that most Americans are unaware of its purpose. Credit scores determine risk. They are used by lenders, insurance and utility companies, and employers for risk management. Lenders would like to know the probability of losses for a loan. Insurance companies want a current indicator of future claims. Utilities would like to know the possibility of unpaid services. Employers use scores for job applicants to detect any concerns for theft or embezzlement.

For lenders, credit scores first arrived on the scene in 1995. They were used primarily as a guide and not as the sole credit factor in determining loan approval. As years have gone by, credit scores have practically become both the sole determining factor in a credit decision and the interest rate on every loan. Even one point can result in a loan or insurance coverage denial, or a higher interest rate or insurance premium. The question is, *"How much does our credit score cost us?"*

1

Cost of a Credit Score

1st Mortgage

200,000 Loan / 30 Year Fixed Interest Rates

Range of Credit Scores	Interest Rate	Monthly Payments	Extra Mo. Cost	Total Extra Cost
760 to **850**	6.33%	$1,235	- 0 -	- 0 -
700 to **759**	6.55%	$1,263	$18	$10,253
680 to **699**	6.73%	$1,287	$52	$18,713
660 to **679**	6.95%	$1,316	$81	$29,135
640 to **659**	7.38%	$1,374	$139	$49,766
620 to **639**	7.92%	$1,447	$212	$76,140

Interest rates as of June 2006.

2nd Mortgage

$50,000 / 15 Year Home Equity Loan

Range of Credit Scores	Interest Rate	Monthly Payments	Extra Mo. Cost	Total Extra Cost
720 to **850**	8.00%	$475	- 0 -	- 0 -
700 to **719**	8.13%	$478	$3	$664
680 to **699**	8.63%	$493	$18	$3,236
660 to **679**	8.75%	$496	$21	$3,861
640 to **659**	9.00%	$503	$28	$5,166
620 to **639**	10.50%	$548	$73	$13,183

Interest rates as of June 2006.

The Cost

Mortgage and auto interest rates, and insurance premiums vary throughout the country. However, a quick glimpse and we can see the impact of our credit scores. Even when we are charged a higher interest rate on a loan or an insurance premium from a lower credit score, the chances are very slim that we will be able to refinance that loan or lower our insurance premium for years. Unless we take steps to improve our credit score, it could cost us literally thousands of dollars annually.

Many lenders advertise their mortgage interest rates based upon ranges of credit scores. Even though interest rates can vary throughout the country, the differences are startling. If we compare two people, one

Cost of a Credit Score

Homeowner's Insurance
$250,000 / $500 Deductible Standard Coverage / No Recent Claims

Range of Credit Scores	Annual Premiums	Extra Monthly Cost	Extra Annual Cost
720 to 850	$554	- 0 -	- 0 -
700 to 719	$590	$3	$36
680 to 699	$703	$12	$149
660 to 679	$737	$15	$183
640 to 659	$737	$15	$183
620 to 639	$923	$31	$369
580 to 619	$1,219	$55	$665
Below 579	$1,476	$77	$922

Auto Insurance
$20,000 Auto / $500 Deductible Standard Coverage / No Recent Claims

Range of Credit Scores	Annual Premiums	Extra Monthly Cost	Extra Annual Cost
720 to 850	$326	- 0 -	- 0 -
700 to 719	$348	$2	$22
680 to 699	$379	$4	$53
660 to 679	$499	$14	$173
640 to 659	$517	$16	$191
620 to 639	$600	$23	$274
580 to 619	$654	$27	$328
Below 579	$754	$36	$428

Insurance premiums based on home and auto in the Salt Lake City / Ogden Utah areas as of June 2006.
Insurance premiums vary from state to state, city to city, and from company to company.

with a credit score of 625 credit score and the second with 765, the extra payment in this analysis would be $212 a month on a $200,000 mortgage. Over the life of this loan, the total cost would be an additional $76,410. According to this analysis, a 725 credit score could cost an extra $28 a month. We may be charged a higher interest rate on a first mortgage even with a credit score below 760.

Second mortgages follow the lead of first mortgages and advertise interest rates based on credit scores. We can go to many websites or contact lenders personally to compare interest rates for second mortgages, auto and personal loans, and credit cards. The lower the credit score, the higher the interest rate and monthly payment. The extra cost can be substantial for each type of loan.

Before we apply for any loan, we should find out the actual interest rate. Lenders usually advertise their best interest rates via television, radio, or internet for those who have a 760 or higher credit score. If we have a lower credit score, we may be surprised by the actual interest rate when we sign the loan papers.

Insurance Companies

Insurance companies have just recently adjusted premiums according to credit scores. We may pay a higher home, auto, and life insurance premium because of a lower score even though we have never have had an insurance claim. We may be unaware of the higher premium unless we inquire. Insurance companies insist that credit scores help them predict the number of future claims.

This issue is a hot topic with state and local governments. Many national, state, and local legislators contend that such policies are discriminatory against those less fortunate. This issue will be fought through Congress, state legislatures, and the courts over the coming years before a final determination is made. Some companies have changed their systems in determining premiums as a result of the political fallout. They now use what they call, *'insurance scores.'* In many cases they are still based on the credit scoring models.

Those insurance companies that are still not using credit scores to determine their premiums will eventually be forced into using them. If credit scores do predict future insurance claims, companies that charge higher premiums for those with lower credit scores can offset substantial losses from higher premiums. On the other hand, insurance companies offering lower premiums to those with poorer credit scores could expect additional losses.

Additional Applications

More employers are also reviewing credit scores for possible employment. Even the military uses them for advancement in rank. Electrical, phone, gas, and other utility companies may soon jump in after regulatory approval and give discounts for those with higher scores. The use of credit scores continues to expand and those on the lower end could eventually find additional costs for future basic services.

As additional situations arise in our life now and into the future, the cost of a lower credit score could continue to rise. Therefore, we should make an extra effort to understand the credit scoring system along with a consistent effort to improve our scores. We can raise our scores so that we can qualify for the best terms on any financial transaction in the future. Our scores should be sufficiently high enough so that they cannot hold us back from any employment possibilities. As we travel the road to 850, we will find many additional savings or earning possibilities if we only make the necessary changes now.

Understanding a Credit Report

Credit scores are determined by some, but not all, of the information contained in our credit report. Since each credit report has it own distinct language, understanding the information can seem like we're reading the Japanese language upside down. Unless the language within a credit report is somewhat mastered, it is almost impractical to understand. We may become frustrated and eventually give up trying to comprehend it. Given that there are not a lot of available dictionaries for a credit report, understanding it can be extremely challenging. Identifying the important elements in our report is critical to increasing our credit scores. Let's take a moment to review our credit report.

Credit Agencies or Bureaus:	Equifax, Experian, & Trans Union *(Three Major Credit Bureaus)*
Credit Files:	Each credit bureau establishes a credit file through information from various sources. There are three separate credit files for each person — one from each major credit bureau.
Credit Reports:	A commentary of the information in a credit file is provided by the credit bureaus in the form of a credit report to lenders, insurers, landlords, employers, and individuals.
Credit Report Sections:	There are separate sections of the credit report: Personal information, credit summary *(optional)*, credit scores *(optional)*, satisfactory and derogatory accounts, inquiries, public records, and credit bureau information.

Credit Files

The three major credit agencies, *Experian*, *Equifax*, and *Trans Union* create individual credit files on each of us by gathering information from multiple sources. Personal credit files are then generated from the information gathered from their sources, and are released in the form of a credit report. Each agency usually does not share its acquired information with the other two major credit bureaus. Therefore, we can have three very different credit reports.

The information in our credit file includes legal name, social security number, birthday, gender, present and any former home addresses, present and past employers, bankruptcies, tax liens, judgments, collections, present and past lenders, loan information, and inquiries. When we request a copy of our credit report, it simply reflects all the information gathered in our individual credit files from the credit bureau's sources such as lenders, court houses, and collection agencies. Some credit files may be newly created, while others may have dozens of references.

A credit report is produced when the information in our credit file is requested by companies or ourselves. Credit agencies have no one standard legible form when a credit report is provided. This makes it challenging to read them. Since the information in each credit report may be different and reported in multiple unique forms, we can have difficulty understanding all its information.

Credit reports are usually divided into several main sections: personal information, credit summary *(optional)*, credit scores *(optional)*, account and collection information, inquiries, public records, and credit bureau information. The information gathered by the agencies into the credit file and reported in the credit report, whether correct or incorrect, generates our credit scores. Some areas of the credit report are of more concern than others. Let's review the individual sections.

Personal Information

The personal information section of the credit report generally does not directly impact credit scores. This section simply identifies the person in the credit file with a legal name (including any variations), social security number, birth date, former and current addresses, and former and current employers. The personal information in this section has been gathered by the agencies from creditors who have either reported our information from a loan or have requested a credit report. The information we give creditors at loan application is usually the information that is reflected in this section of our credit report.

Personal Information

Name:	John Doe
Social Security Number:	111-11-1111
Birth Date:	January 1, 1960

Current Address:
123 Any Road
Any Town, USA 11111

Previous Address:
456 One Road
One Town, USA 22222

This information is used primarily for identification purposes. Review the name and social security number for accuracy. Otherwise, the information contained in this section does not directly impact credit scores.

Current Employment:
ZYX Corporation

We may often find the information in this section as old or inaccurate. When names, addresses, or employers are incorrectly entered by lenders, this misinformation will usually reflect in the personal information section of the credit file. Lenders don't always update their own files. They may continue to communicate incorrect information to the credit bureaus for years. Additionally, different spellings of names and addresses are often reflected in this personal section.

Robert bought an anniversary ring for his wife and took out a loan to finance the purchase. He used his work as a mailing address for the monthly billing so that his wife would not find out the true cost of the ring. When he received a copy of his credit report a year later, Robert was surprised to discover that his credit report was listing his work address as his primary residence. Since he listed his work as his billing address for the ring, the lender simply passed this information along to the credit bureau as his primary residence.

Any variations in name, social security number, or address can create misinformation and possibly even a duplicate credit file. Common inaccuracies can occur with similar names from father and son, or twins. We should use one legal name and address that no one else uses for all credit transactions to hopefully avoid any possible mistakes or duplication in our credit file.

Credit Summary

The credit summary section is full of valuable information that can impact scores. Not all credit reports however have a credit summary section. Nevertheless, it contains the overall breakdown of the information found in the credit report. This section lists the inquiries, the total number of accounts in the file, loan balances, open and closed loans, along with the number of accounts paid *'Satisfactory'* and ones that have had late payments. It also lists the number of account types such as mortgage, installment, and revolving accounts reporting in the file, along with the current balances and the number of late payments.

The total number of mortgage, installment, or revolving accounts (called trade lines) represents the total accounts reported in the credit report, even if they have been paid off and closed. The balances reveal the current debt owed with each type of loan. The payments are the current total of monthly payments reflected in the credit report. The limits are the total high credit limits for revolving loans and the total initial loan amounts for installment loans. The 30 / 60 / 90 day late payments indicate the number of past due payments with each type of account in the credit report. It also reports how late the payments were made; 30 (meaning 30 days past due the payment due date or one payment overdue), 60 (meaning 60 days past due the payment due date or two payments overdue) and a 90 (meaning 90 days past due the due date or three payments past due). In the given example, one 30 day late payment is reported from a revolving account. It does not identify the loan in the credit summary. We must review our report to find that account.

Credit Summary

Type of Account	Payments	Total Balance	Limits
Mortgage	$1,319	$174,310	$185,000
Installment	$491	$15,318	$15,500
Revolving	$181	$4,911	$10,000
Total Accounts	$1,991	$194,539	$210,500

Type of Account	No of Accounts	30	60	90
Mortgage	3	0	0	0
Installment	5	0	0	0
Revolving	4	1	0	0
Total Accounts	12	1	0	0

Number of Open Accounts *(currently)*:	7
Number of Closed Accounts:	5
Total Accounts in Good Standing / Satisfactory:	11
Inquiries in Last 12 Months:	6
Accounts Currently Past Due:	0
Negative Account History:	1
Public Record:	0
Bankruptcies:	0

The areas highlighted in red directly affect credit scores and should be given attention.

We should review this summary for accuracy. It does not contain every vital piece of information for credit scores. Nevertheless, we can review the information in this section to identify areas of concern and make improvements that influence our credit scores.

Credit Scores

Credit scores may or may not be provided with a credit report because it is a source of revenue for the credit bureaus. If a free credit report is requested from one of the credit bureaus, the score is usually not provided unless paid for by the recipient. Even if the credit score is requested, the score given will probably not be the same one used by a particular lender or insurance company.

The credit scores are the summation of all the information gathered into the credit file. The three credit scores represent the information contained in the *Experian* credit file, the *Equifax* credit file, and the *Trans Union* credit file. Since the information in each credit file varies and credit agencies use their own exclusive scoring models, the three credit scores are almost always different. The three scores are usually within 30 points of each other, but they can sometimes be even 100 or more points apart.

Additionally, lenders do not always use the same credit score. One lender may use only one particular score such as the *FICO* (Experian), while another lender may use the middle of all three scores. Therefore, it is important to keep tabs on all three credit scores.

Credit scores are discussed further in Chapter 3.

Account Information *(Includes collections)*

The account information section is the nuts and bolts of the credit report and has a considerable influence on our scores. This section identifies those creditors we currently have or have had outstanding loans in the last seven years. It discloses all satisfied, derogatory, and collection accounts. Some credit reports even break down the satisfied and derogatory accounts into separate individual sections.

The account information section discloses all the information on lenders, the account numbers, the opening and last reporting dates for each loan, the high credit limits and the balances, the last active dates for each account, the monthly payments, any current amount past due, the types of account, payment history and any late payments for up to seven years. A brief explanation is provided for this sub-section of the credit report.

Account Name

The account name is the lender of record on the credit file for each loan. Lenders may appear in our credit report under different and often unfamiliar names or symbols. The type of lender we use can impact our credit scores. Some lenders are more valuable to scores than others. Additionally, we may not find each lender in all three credit reports. Many lenders report to all three major credit bureaus while others may only report to one credit bureau, if at all. Our accounts usually stay on the credit report for seven years after the last active date.

Account Number

Account numbers are the figures used for identification purposes by the lender for a particular loan. The account number is oftentimes truncated or partially reported on the credit report to prevent identity theft. Since they are used primarily for identification purposes, account numbers do not impact our credit scores.

Open Date

The open date is the month and year we have opened a loan with a lender. Since the length of time active accounts are open is a significant

Account Information

Creditor Acct No.	Rptg Date	Open Date	Active Date	High Credit	Balance	Payment	Past Due	Pmt Type	Hist
DEF Bank 1234	1/06	12/02	1/06	185,000	174,310	1319	0	Mtg	ccccccccccc ccccccccccc
RST Auto 4567	1/06	10/05	1/06	15,500	15,318	491	0	Ins	ccc
HIJ Card 7890	1/06	3/00	1/06	3,000	2,871	66	0	Rev	ccccccccccc c1ccccccccccc (12/04 –1)
JKL Card 1122	1/06	7/03	1/06	2,000	1,040	43	0	Rev	ccccccccccc ccccccccccc
CDE Card 3344	1/06	4/98	1/06	1,500	540	20	0	Rev	ccccccccccc ccccccccccc
LO Bank 5566	1/06	4/05	1/06	1,000	460	16	0	Rev	ccccccccc
123 CU 1234	1/06	2/03	9/05	1,000	0	0	0	Rev	xxxcccccxcc ccccccccccc

The areas highlighted in red directly affect credit scores and should be given attention.

calculation in our credit scores, this date reported by our lenders to the credit bureaus is important.

If a loan is newly opened, refinanced, or transferred, a new account is usually established. A new open date will be reported reflecting a recent month and year *(1/06 means January 2006)*. Even if an account has been open for many years and is refinanced, there is a good chance that a new loan will be set up with a recent opening date.

Reporting Date

The reporting date is the last month and year a lender reported account information to the credit bureaus. Since the information reported to the credit file impacts our credit scores, it is important for us to track these reporting dates. Creditors usually stop reporting loan information to the credit bureaus when the loan is paid off and closed, or an account has been sent to collection.

We can usually identify those accounts that are open and active by tracking the reporting dates. Those loans that have a recent month and year as a reporting date are usually still open. Closed loans have a re-porting date that is months or years old and or state *'Closed loan'* under the account number. If we have a question, we may have to contact the lender to verify if a loan is still open.

Last Active Date or Status Date

The last active date also has a significant influence on credit scores. This column identifies the last month and year the account had any loan or payment activity. Even if a revolving account is open, it may have a minimal impact on scores if there is no recent loan activity. We must always demonstrate an ongoing ability to borrow and pay back on satis-factory terms.

When we have a collection or an account with late payments, we can determine the exact month when the account will drop by calculating seven years past the last active date. Accounts usually drop off the credit report seven years after the last active date. For example, a loan has a last active date of 2/02 or February 2002. If the loan is closed, it will remain on the credit report until February 2009 or seven years after the last active date. If an account remains open, this account can remain active and stay on the credit report indefinitely unless closed by either the creditor or the borrower.

Credit Limit *or* High Credit Limit

The high credit limit has a substantial influence on scores for all loans. For revolving loans, lenders usually report the highest range of available credit offered to us. For mortgage (non-revolving loan) and installment loans, the high credit limit reported is the initial loan amount or highest loan balance at anytime the loan has been outstanding. It determines how we have utilized our current accounts by keeping balances low on our credit cards and other revolving accounts, and how much we have paid down on our mortgage, auto or other installment loans.

Balance

The balance can have a sizeable impact on credit scores since both the number of accounts with balances and the amount of each loan balance can impact credit scores. The loan balance is the amount owed on the loan when it was last reported by the lender to the bureau. The last month and year that the balance was communicated to the credit bureau is reflected by the lender's reporting date.

Past Due

Any amount in the past due section on an account is reflected as past due by the last month and year of the reporting date. This amount could be a late fee, past due payments, or even a collection. Any amount in this column has a considerable impact on credit scores since it shows that our payments are currently behind.

Monthly Payment *and* Terms

Monthly payments show the amount of each payment on each loan or the last payment made to the account. In addition, the term or length of the loan may also be reflected. This amount of the payment does not have any direct impact on credit scores.

Payment History — 30 / 60 / 90

The payment history reflects a month by month payment analysis made on the loan during the prior 24 months from the last reporting date. It also reports any late payments on all accounts for up to seven years. If there have been late payments, the month and year of those late payments is reported along with the number of payments the account was past due at that time. This section of the credit report has an extensive impact on our credit scores.

For example, an account with one late payment in January 2006 *(1/06 - 2)* will reflect as a 30-day late payment in the credit file. If the loan continues to show a second 30 day late payment the next month, the credit report reflects 2 - 30 day late payments *(2/06 - 1 and 1/06 - 1)*. If that account was two payments past due in January 2006, the report shows the loan as having 1 - 60 day late *(1/06 - 2)*. If that account was three payments past due, it would show a 90 day late payment *(1/06 - 3)*.

A collection is an account that is at least six months of payments past due or is an account charged off the books of a lender. Such accounts usually reflect a *'9'* or *(1/06 - 9)*. Collections have an extensive influence on credit scores for several years.

When late payments are reflected in the account summary, we should recognize those loans which are reporting late payments. Mistakes do happen. For that reason, we should make a constant effort to review each loan's payment history in our credit report.

Loan Type

A loan is usually listed to the credit bureaus as: Mortgage *'Mtg'*, installment *'Ins'*, or revolving *'Rev'*. A mortgage is secured by real estate and can be either an installment or a revolving loan. An installment account has consistent monthly payments throughout the loan until the balance is paid off. The monthly payments may change, but there is always a monthly payment until the loan is paid in full. Installment loans include mortgage, auto, education, and personal loans. *(See Chapter 8)*

A revolving loan has a payment based on the current balance and interest rate, and can remain open indefinitely. They include home equity loans, credit cards, checking account overdrafts, and personal lines of credit. A proper mixture of installment and revolving loans is important to increasing our credit scores. *(See Chapter 7)*

Inquiries

The section of the credit report that lists those companies that have pulled a our credit report in the last 24 months is listed in *'Inquiries'*. Each inquire identifies the exact date and all the companies that have requested our credit report. Inquires can also have an effect on credit scores. *(See Chapter 4)*

Public Records

Bankruptcies, judgments, and federal and state tax liens show up under the public records section in the credit report. The bankruptcy type, the dates of filing and discharge are reported for each bankruptcy. Judgments show the amount owed, the status *(Satisfied / Unsatisfied)* of the judgment and the plaintiff. Tax liens report the amount owed, the status of the lien *(Paid / Unpaid)* and the type of tax lien *(Federal / State / Local)*.

Any public record in a report has an extensive influence on credit scores for many years. *(See Chapter 11)*

Credit Bureau Information

The last section identifies the credit bureaus used to provide the credit report. It usually provides the addresses and phone numbers to correspond with the credit bureaus along with our rights under the *Fair Credit Reporting Act.* This section provides us the means to contact the credit bureau with any questions we may have, or to file a dispute to correct an inaccuracy.

Delinquent Accounts

There is an additional section that may appear in our credit report. It is called, *"Delinquent accounts"*. This section helps us identify all the loans that have had any late payments or on which we have failed to make satisfactory payments. It also lists those loans that have been sent to a collection company. The number of delinquent accounts has a substantial influence on our credit scores.

An account may have had one 30 day late payment six years ago and still appear in this section. Once an loan has had a late payment, it will show up in this section for seven years from the last late payment. In some instances, the account may remain in this section of the report even after the seven years when the lender or the credit agency fails to remove the account.

When we understand each section of the credit report, we can better understand the information reported. It is like having the road map available when we go on a road trip. We can identify those issues impacting our scores and make faster course corrections. We can also better distinguish any errors within our report. Knowing our credit report is critical to increase our credit scores.

3

Credit Scores and Reason Codes

In order to increase credit scores, we must understand how they are calculated. Scores are derived from a variety of factors. They include payment history, the number of accounts open and with balances, and the length and types of current accounts. We should have a broad understanding of each major factor that impacts our scores.

When a credit report is issued for a company, each credit bureau produces a credit score. However, lenders have a choice which scoring model they want to use. There are two primary credit score models with a third prospective one on the way. Similar to a software program that has an upgrade every couple of years, the credit bureaus keep updating their credit scores to produce a new scoring model. Each model can produce a credit score that is considerably different.

Classic, NextGen, and Vantage

The initial model called the *Classic* model was first introduced in 1995 to the general public when the mortgage investors Fannie Mae and Freddie Mac endorsed the system to assist them in approving mortgage loans. The *Classic* model is produced by *Fair Isaac Co.* and is still offered by the credit bureaus and used by many lenders. Even though there are other scoring models, the *Classic* model is the basis for the other credit scoring models.

A subsequent model was introduced by *Fair Isaac Co.* called *NextGen*. This model was offered by the major credit agencies in 2001. According to *Fair Isaac,* the *NextGen* model is more forgiving on small collections, multiple inquiries, time to establish a credit score, and the use of finance companies as lenders. In many cases we reviewed, the *NextGen* model appears to be more lenient and credit scores can be substantially higher than the *Classic* credit score model. The difference could be up-wards of 50 to 60 points. In multiple cases reviewed, credit scores were 60 to 70 points higher using the *NextGen* score model versus the *Classic* credit score. To this day, the *NextGen* model, however, has never been endorsed or used by either Fannie Mae or Freddie Mac. Since Fannie Mae and Freddie Mac usually set the standards for home mortgages, many lenders follow their lead.

The third and newest model proposed in March 2006 is the *Vantage* credit scoring system offered by *Vantage score* instead of *Fair Isaac Corp.* This model proposes three distinct changes to the credit scoring system. First, the three scoring models differ slightly from one credit bureau to another. The *Vantage* proposal would have the identical scoring system for all three credit bureaus. There would still may be different scores because each credit agency has different information.

Second, the scoring would change. Instead of a range between 300 to 850, this scoring system would provide a score between 500 and 990. A score between 900 and 990 would be an 'A', 800 to 899 would be a 'B', 700 to 799 would be a 'C', 600 to 699 would be a 'D', and 500 to 599 would be an 'F'.

Credit Scores

Classic Model   Scores range between 300 to 850
Industry standard — used by Fannie Mae and Freddie Mac and most mortgage lenders.

Bureau	Credit Score Name	Score
Equifax	*Beacon*	683
Trans Union	*Classic / Emperica*	671
Experian	*FICO*	676

NextGen Model   Scores range between 300 to 850
Used by many retail lenders, insurance companies, and employers.

Bureau	Credit Score Name	Score
Equifax	*Pinnacle*	706
Trans Union	*Precision*	693
Experian	*Advanced FICO*	701

Vantage Model   Scores range between 500 to 990
Proposed new credit score model. Awaiting substantive industry approval as of December 2006.

Third, the makeup of the credit score would change. There would be one additional factor with a greater emphasis than the current credit score models. This issue not only looks at the balances owing, but also the total amount of credit to which we have access. This model may be endorsed and used by the major credit agencies and lenders in the future after an extensive review.

As demonstrated by the *NextGen* scoring model, nothing is for certain unless the major lenders or investors endorse the new system. Even if the *Vantage* model is approved by the lending industry, the changes in the system could take several months, or even years before we would start seeing them used.

Versions

Many loan officers and consumers are unaware that there are differing versions of each scoring model. For example, there could be version A, B, or C that a lender could use from *Equifax* for the *Classic* score model. We could go to two different lenders who both use the *Classic* credit score model and discover that the credit scores are slightly different. One lender could use version A while the second lender could use version B. When a lender tells us our score is 680, we could go home

Credit Scores

Classic Model

Equifax   *(Beacon)* 683

10	Proportion of balances to credit limits too high on revolving balances.
9	Too many accounts recently opened.
14	Length of time accounts have been established.
5	Too many accounts with balances.

Trans Union   *(Classic – can also be called Emperica)* 671

9	Too many accounts recently opened.
10	Proportion of revolving balances to revolving credit limits is too high.
5	Too many accounts with balances.
11	Amount owed on revolving accounts is too high.

Experian   *(FICO)* 676

10	Proportion of balances to high credit on revolving accounts.
11	Amount owed on revolving accounts.
5	Number of accounts with balances.
14	Time since oldest trade line established.

and pull our credit score online from the bureaus and find a 693 score. The difference in credit scores between the versions should be no more than ten to 15 points. The differences are tailored to distinctive lenders such as mortgage, auto, and credit card. Employers and insurance companies also use their own scoring models.

When we are asked what our credit score is, we can simply reply, *"Which credit score?"* Since there are so many models, we should track our credit score from one particular source to help us recognize any upward or downward movements. Otherwise, we may think our credit score is going higher when in fact the difference may simply be another version.

The type of financing often determines the credit score model used. Since the *Classic* model is used for mortgage lending and is the basis for the other models, this publication highlights this credit scoring system. Any changes found in the *NextGen* scoring model are noted throughout this publication.

Reason Codes

With the *Classic* credit score model, there are over 30 risk factors commonly referred to as '*Reason codes*' or '*Primary drivers*'. These codes highlight the different risk factors from various credit situations. They are used by the credit bureaus to convert our credit risk into that all-important three digit number. Identifying the meaning of all the codes offers all of us a chance to better understand the credit scoring system and to increase our scores.

The major credit bureaus provide very limited explanations to the general public by way of these reason codes. There are even confidentiality agreements so that the makeup of this system is not publicly disclosed. The general reasoning for this is attributed to the proprietary nature of the system.

From our research and experience on credit scores, we are able to provide some guidance into the acceptable ranges of credit risk. These ranges include the number of accounts open, the number of loans with balances, how often to open new loans, when to close loans, lenders that add value, and lenders to avoid. We also provide some guidance on acceptable balances on our credit cards and other revolving accounts, and our mortgage and auto loans.

All three of the credit score models and credit bureaus use basically the same primary factors to determine credit scores. The variances in the credit scores comes from differences in the weight each credit agency gives to each primary factor. One credit agency may weigh one factor more than another model which can produce a slightly different score.

When we receive a copy of our credit scores from the three major bureaus, a lender, or *Fair Isaac Corporation* (MyFICO), they are usually given with four or five corresponding numbers and general explanations. Even though the reason codes can vary with each credit bureau, the top four reason codes listed are considered to have the greatest negative impact for that particular score according to that specific bureau. They sometimes come in different layouts or explanations. However, these explanations are critical to recognize those factors that are hurting our credit score with that credit agency.

These codes and explanations are the primary drivers to the credit scoring system. We can have a few factors, or can have many factors, influencing scores. Because of its proprietary nature, the credit bureaus only disclose the top four or five concerns. The lower number of overall factors affecting scores, the higher the credit score and vice versa.

This credit scoring system is similar to a road trip. When we go on a long trip to visit a particular location in a city, we may never find a particular location unless a map, directions, or road signs are provided. These items are necessary to help us arrive at a given destination.

Like driving in a foreign country, not all the road signs are similar to those we see in the United States. There may be different signs for

speed limit, direction, exiting or entering a freeway, stop, or even traffic lights. By identifying and understanding the road signs and then following directions, we can go in the right direction to safely arrive at a particular destination.

The reason codes are the directional signs provided by credit bureaus to help us increase our scores. Even though they can be difficult to understand at times, these generic explanations are critically important. Once understood, some course corrections can have immediate results. Other factors may take months or even years for course correction to arrive on the right path.

Identifying the reason codes, understanding the corresponding risk factors with explanations, and following directions are all critical to charting the correct course and to increasing our credit scores. We can then make better decisions and plans to enhance our scores. By understanding, planning, and by creating short and long term strategies, we can better manage our credit and more easily increase scores to an 800 level within a shorter period of time.

For more information on these reason codes, please see Appendix A. We have provided the reason codes used by mortgage lenders from the *Classis* credit score model with a brief explanation for each factor.

Credit Score Strategies

Chapters 4 thru 13

◆━━━━━━━━━━━━━━━━━━━━━━━━━━━━━━━━━━━━━━━◆

We are often looking for ways to increase our credit scores. There are many theories. As we learn about the credit scoring system, we can identify several strategies to help improve our score. One strategy, however, for one particular person may not be the best strategy for another. Everyone's credit situation varies. The more correct information we have now, the better chance we can improve our credit rating and secure the best terms in the future.

These strategies have been used for several years and are means to help us increase our credit scores. We can quickly discover those matters of concern and the direction we should follow to increase our credit scores. These strategies are given in the following chapters. The chapters are called: *Inquiries, Developing Credit, Quality Credit, Revolving Accounts, Installment Loans, Credit Management, Common Errors, Late Payments, Danger Zone,* and *Identity Theft.*

The reason codes are referenced throughout the subsequent chapters. Unless otherwise noted, the reason codes in most instances provided is Equifax's Beacon score. For a complete list of the reason codes from each bureau, please go to Addendum A.

Inquiries

The credit bureaus gather information from many lenders to create a personal credit file. Our legal name (or any variance), addresses, birth date, social security number, and employment history all reflect our information that many companies have shared with the credit bureaus. Companies exchange our information with the credit bureaus upon a formal request for a credit report or to report account information.

Credit bureaus have contractual agreements with lenders, insurers, landlords, employers, marketing firms, among others, to exchange information when requesting a credit report or updating an account. Our information can be requested by many companies, with or without our authorization and even without our knowledge. Companies pay the credit bureaus to retrieve information from our personal credit files to determine any services they may want to offer us.

"To investigate: to seek information about" is the Webster's New World Dictionary's official explanation of an inquire. Companies are simply investigating or requesting additional information about us before they agree to offer a particular service. They want to have a better understanding and determine the likelihood that we will default on a loan, have a claim, or create additional risk at a place of employment. What is the potential financial cost if they give us a loan, insure us, or offer us a job? They are taking a risk that can possibly cost them financially. They want to determine that possibility to reduce their costs by gathering more information on us from our credit report.

Every time one of these companies request a copy of our credit report, an inquiry appears. Similar to any monetary transaction, a record is maintained by each of the three major credit bureaus and stored in our individual credit files. This record identifies those entities that have requested our credit report in the last 24 months. Inquiries are the first

Inquiries		
Companies	**Date**	**Credit Bureau**
EFG Financial	01/04/2006	EFX
JIH Bank	01/07/2006	TU
JIH Bank	01/07/2006	EFX
JIH Bank	01/07/2006	XPN
RST Marketing	01/21/2006	XPN
WXY Employment Services	01/30/2006	EFX

signals to credit bureaus and to creditors that we are taking on new debt. This raises our level of risk and ultimately affect our scores. According to *Fair Isaac Corporation*, those of us with six or more inquiries in our credit report are eight times more likely to file a bankruptcy than someone who has no inquiries.

As a society, we love to purchase new homes, cars, computers, televisions and other expensive items. Our behavior generally leads to more expensive items from month to month, and year to year. In order to keep up with the Joneses', we often finance many of these purchases. As long as we can make the monthly payments, we believe that there will never be a problem.

Our credit report is usually requested by a prospective lender every time we apply for financing. This request creates an inquiry. Lenders will then review our past credit performance and check our credit scores. Upon each request, a record appears in the inquiry section of our credit files which identifies the company requesting the report, the type of inquiry, the date, and the credit bureau.

One or two inquiries in a year has a minimal effect on credit scores while multiple inquiries can have a much greater impact. *"Too many inquiries in the last 12 months"* (8) appears when a credit file has an excessive number of inquiries that is negatively impacting scores. The greater number of inquiries, the more impact on scores.

There is however a couple of exceptions to these rules. There are those inquiries that impact credit scores and others that do not. Some inquiries are generated from a request to receive a free copy of our credit report. Other inquiries come from current lenders evaluating our account, insurance companies assessing premiums, or an employer examining a our job application. There are situations when multiple inquiries only count as one inquiry even though multiple lenders have requested our report. We need to have a good understanding of inquiries to limit their impact on our scores.

1. Track Our Credit Scores

Ask for scores when applying for credit

We miss a great opportunity to recognize pressing concerns when our credit reports are requested. One of the greatest opportunities to discover information about our scores is when a lender requests a copy of our credit report. Asking for our credit scores and requesting their corresponding credit risk factors help us identify those areas of concern.

The three credit scores will usually appear at the beginning of our credit report. Each credit bureau will only provide their respective credit score if that bureau's credit file has been requested as part of the report. Scores will show up under different names with the *Classic* model: *Equifax* has '*Beacon*', *Experian* has '*FICO*', and *Trans Union* has '*Classic*' or '*Emperica*'. As previously revealed, the three scores in most instances vary from one to another. In addition, the scoring models (*Classic, NextGen, or Vantage*) used by each lender may differ. Since lenders may use all three scores, we should track each score.

When trying to access this information, most of us discover that scores are not readily available. Not every credit report reveals our credit scores. We soon discover that we must usually pay a fee for our scores when requesting a free copy of our credit report. Otherwise, the credit bureaus will send a report void of the scores. In other instances, knock-off or counterfeit scores may be given.

Mortgage lenders usually use a different credit score model than a credit card or insurance company. Since companies often use different credit score models, we should chose one preferred source to track our scores. We could track our score from a preferred lender or from *www.MyFICO.com*. Each lender generally uses the same credit score model. We can then more clearly track the progress of our credit scores when we reference one source. As we track our scores, we can recognize our true direction and better identify the means to improve them.

When we fail to know our credit scores along with the codes, we are like a boat without a rudder going in no real direction. We should take every opportunity to know our scores and identify ways to improve them. By requesting this information at loan application from our preferred lender or check periodically online, we can better track and understand how to improve our scores. Always ask when applying for a loan even if we use another source to track our scores. A simple request can lead to a wealth of knowledge, and knowledge is power.

2. Types of Inquiries

Differentiate between 'Hard' and 'Soft' inquiries

As we review the inquiries in our credit report, we may notice several unfamiliar companies that have requested our credit report. Such companies may include other lenders, insurance agencies, employers, and marketing firms. Every request for our credit report shows as an inquiry, but not all inquiries impact our credit scores. Understanding the differences can help us identify those inquiries that impact our scores.

There are two types of inquiries on our credit report and they impact credit scores differently. *'Hard'* inquiries affect credit scores while *'soft'* inquiries do not. An application for a new loan or to raise a credit limit usually results in a hard inquiry when the lender requests a credit report. Requests by banks, credit unions, mortgage lenders, education loans, credit card companies, merchant accounts, and auto dealers almost always result in a hard inquiry on our credit report. When *"Too many recent inquiries"* (8) appears as a warning sign with our credit score, we have had too many hard inquiries in the last 12 months.

A soft inquiry on the other hand occurs when a company requests a credit report for marketing, account reviews, employment, and insurance. A soft inquiry also occurs when we request a copy of our free credit report. Soft inquiries are not necessarily part of a loan application and can even occur without our knowledge or authorization. A credit card company may purchase our credit report for a pre-approved credit offer, or for an account review. An employer may request a credit score before hiring us, or an insurance company may use a credit score to determine an auto insurance premium. In many of these instances, we may not realize our credit report and score have been requested.

Some credit reports separate inquiries into sections: marketing, account review, and credit application. Those inquiries from credit applications are generally the ones that impact scores. Multiple hard inquiries for credit affect our credit scores if they occurred within the last year. The *Inquiries* section in our credit report shows when and how often our credit report has been requested. We should track the number of hard inquiries with each of the three credit bureaus. By recognizing those inquiries that affect our scores, we can space the number of requests for our credit report and limit the impact from too many hard inquiries on our scores.

Classifications

Each company pulling a credit report and providing credit information is given a classification by the credit bureaus to determine the type of lender (also found in Chapter 6). They determine whether an inquiry is a *hard* or *soft* inquiry, and the quality of lender. Bureaus only provide this information in the inquiries section of some credit reports. They classify for *hard* or *soft* inquiries in the credit report, and for lenders according to their reason codes. There are dozens of classifications. These are the more relevant classifications.

Company	Explanation
Bank	Banks are federal or state banks. They do auto loans, credit cards, overdraft accounts, and home equity loans.
Mortgage Company	They include those that finance residential mortgages such as *National City Mortgage*, *Wells Fargo Mortgage*, and *Countrywide*.
Department Store	Department stores include *Sears*, *JCPenney*, *Mervyns*, and other large retail outlets.
Finance Company	Finance companies are sometimes difficult to recognize. They are high risk lenders and are given their own classification.
Finance Company *(Variations)*	Other lenders are considered variations of finance companies. They do not punish scores like a true finance company. There are credit unions, and auto lenders to name a few.
Furniture Store	These outlets are considered similar to department stores. They offer in-house financing.
National Credit Card	These are the national companies that offer credit cards nationwide. They include *American Express*, *Capital One*, and *Discover*.
Utilities	Utilities include electric, gas, telephone, and water.
Collection	Collection company accounts include those companies who are collecting a past due bill.
Miscellaneous	Credit agency reviews, pre-approved offers, or personal requests for a credit report.

3. Multiple Inquiries

Limit the number of hard inquiries

Hard inquiries impact credit scores through applications for various loans. When multiple loan applications are made within a 12 month period, numerous hard inquiries turn up in our credit report and they can have a substantial impact on our scores. For that reason, we must limit the number of hard inquiries.

Our credit needs today will not be the same as tomorrow, next month or year. Most everyone takes out a new loan from time to time to pay for items such as new appliances, home or auto repairs, medical expenses, or even a new car. Our needs are constantly changing. Because of these changes, our current loans almost never stay open very long.

While trying to increase a credit score to 800 or higher, we should limit the number of hard inquiries in each individual credit file within the last 12 months. Requests for new loans should be curtailed and established credit accounts should be utilized.

Once we have an established credit file, we should limit the number of hard inquiries to no more than two per year. With two hard inquiries for each of the three credit bureaus, we should total no more than six hard inquiries within the last twelve months. This doesn't mean that a third inquiry will drop a credit score 100 points. Rather, hard inquiries should be spread out between all three credit bureaus to limit their impact. If we have numerous hard inquiries in our credit report, we should avoid additional credit report requests for up to a year.

With those of us who are building credit or who are self-employed, two or less inquiries within a year may be impractical. If we want to rebuild our credit within the next year, a couple of new loans should be suffi-cient to establish and raise our credit score. Those who are self-employed or who are capable consumers should avoid new requests for credit even if monetary discounts are given. A common mistake is to open new loans every month or two.

Whatever our situation, we should make every effort to reduce the num-ber of new loans which has a corresponding impact on the number of hard inquiries. By limiting hard inquiries, credit scores can more easily increase and stay above 800.

4. Loan Application

Review loan terms with lenders before applying

Sometimes we apply for credit with several lenders hoping to find the best terms for a loan. Other times, a loan officer may shop our loan application looking for the best deal, not necessarily for the prospective borrowers, but rather for the loan officer. Either way, numerous loan applications encourage multiple requests for credit reports. This action increases the number of unnecessary hard inquiries and raises the credit risk level, *"Too many inquiries in the last 12 months"* (8).

A direct lender is preferable to an independent broker in reducing the number of hard inquiries. We should locate a quality direct lender and work primarily with them for our auto and mortgage loans. Direct lenders include banks, credit unions, or other companies that loan their own money. Brokers on the other hand take a our application and usually shop the loan application to multiple lenders. This process often leads to multiple requests for our credit report which produces numerous inquiries. Direct lenders usually produce one hard inquiry while independent brokers can generate multiple hard inquiries.

Those of us who want an 800 score or higher must avoid the practice of shopping lenders, or having lenders shop our loan. If we want to find the lowest interest rate and costs for a loan, we should contact several direct lenders and provide them with our credit scores, type of loan, income, and monthly debt. These lenders can then provide a basic outline of loan options for us. Once the interest rate and loan terms have been determined, an educated decision on the best lender can be made before formally applying for the loan. We can usually find the lowest interest rate and best loan terms by utilizing this strategy.

Income, credit scores, and other information can change when all the documentation is provided. Lenders may make adjustments to the loan. However, this method can reduce the number of hard inquiries. This system eliminates a common practice by brokers of shopping our loan which inevitably produces multiple hard inquiries.

With a score in the 700 or 800s, as little as three or more hard inquiries within the last 12 months is usually a top factor impacting a credit score. The higher number of hard inquiries, the greater the negative impact on our scores. By reviewing the loan terms with lenders before applying, we should be able to reduce the number of unnecessary hard inquiries in our credit report.

5. Auto and Mortgage Inquiries

Time given to shop for an auto or mortgage loan

Homes and vehicles are major purchases for which many of us take time to locate the best lender with the lowest interest rate and fees. Small changes in interest rate and loan terms can make substantial differences in monthly payments. The credit bureaus give us time to shop lenders for the best loan terms when financing a new home or auto.

If we do not know a trusted home or auto lender, credit bureaus allow prospective buyers to make multiple applications with minimal impact to credit scores. This exception to the rule allows us time to shop a loan without incurring multiple hard inquiries on our credit report. With the *Classic* risk scoring model, we have 14 days to shop auto and mortgage lenders according to *Fair Isaac*. The *NextGen* model is more forgiving and allows us up to 45 days to find a lender.

With this time, a prospective homeowner or car buyer can apply with several lenders to look for the best loan. Even though there could be multiple requests for our credit report, these inquiries will only count as one hard inquiry if the credit reports from all the mortgage or auto lenders are pulled within the given time frame.

There are however three potential issues to recognize. First, many lender systems are computerized and they review the number of recent inquiries as one of the determining factors for loan approval. Second, our loan may be denied even though the credit score is above acceptable standards if there are multiple inquiries.

Additionally, several mortgage and auto lenders reduce costs by pulling credit reports through third party vendors or use the same systems as their company's credit card or personal loan departments. In such instances, the credit bureaus have difficulty differentiating between the applications of an auto or any other loan. Failure to properly communicate can mean additional hard inquiries.

Loan applicants should ask lenders two questions. First, if the lender pulls a credit report directly or through a third party credit reporting company. Second, if the lender is identified as a mortgage or auto lender to the credit bureaus when requesting credit reports. If they don't know, chances are the lender will pull multiple reports affecting our scores. We may even force the lender to become more educated. By understanding the processes involved and the grace period allowed, we can be reduce the number of hard inquiries on our report.

5
Developing Credit

Many of us look for ways to build our credit so that we can establish a respected credit score. There is generally no quick formula to increase credit scores that takes less than 60 days. Building a credit score takes time and a consistent effort. Making the right decisions now by establishing quality credit references is critical. Creating a credit file under the right circumstances helps us build respectable scores quickly.

Finding opportunities to build quality credit references can be challenging. If we have no credit references, we may have limited opportunities to establish credit to build our credit scores. Even with a poor credit record, trying to find creditors to re-establish credit can be very limited. It can be a vicious cycle. No credit scores, no loan. No loan, no credit scores. It can be a no-win situation.

The *Classic* credit score model requires loan activity for at least six months before a credit score can be established. Both good and bad credit can establish a score as long as there is some loan activity in the last few months. Even if there is a substantial credit history, but there is no loan activity in the last six months, a credit file may have insufficient information to establish a credit score. (According to *Fair Isaac*, the *NextGen* model reduces this time down to three months of loan activity before a credit score is available.) Some people have applied for a loan after they have paid off and closed every account. Their credit score has dropped off entirely because of recent inactivity.

Individual circumstance determines the means available for each of us. The relationship a we have with the local bank or credit union can reveal some opportunities. On the other hand, the local auto dealer is not always one of the preferred places to establish credit. We should review each possibility for its value before opening a loan. The value of a loan and the lender has a lasting impact on our credit scores for several

Types of Lenders

In no particular order

Lenders	Example
1. Mortgage Lenders	*National City Mortgage, Countrywide, Wells Fargo Mortgage*
2. Banks	*Chase, Wells Fargo, Citibank Washington Mutual*
3. National Credit Card Companies	*American Express, Discover, Capital One, Providian*
3. Credit Unions	*Local, not-for-profit*
4. Savings and Loan	*Regional companies*
5. Auto Lenders	*GMAC, Ford, Chrysler, Honda*
6. Department Store Lenders	*Sears, JCPenney, Home Depot*
7. Finance Companies	*Wells Fargo Finance, Citifinancial, American General Finance and Payday Lenders*

years. When we work to build or rebuild a credit file, we should work primarily with those lenders such as banks or national credit card companies which are considered more valuable. Otherwise, the time to increase our scores will take longer.

Within months and perhaps a year or two, we can build respectable credit scores. We will then have more opportunities to establish credit in the future with the best lenders and expect the best rates and terms. We must start now and not wait for another day. If we wait, the longer the time it takes to establish quality scores. Once the door is open, the possibilities for credit can be endless. The challenge is just getting the door open.

6. Unreported Information

Use lenders who report to all three credit bureaus

The three credit scores from the major bureaus are almost never the same. In most cases, the credit files compiled by *Experian, Equifax*, and *Trans Union* have different loan information in each their credit files. Inconsistent reporting is usually traced to lenders who fail to report our account information to all three major credit bureaus. Using lenders that report to all three bureaus is vitally important to build all three scores.

Many smaller credit card, auto, or other lenders often fail to report to three credit bureaus. The cost to exchange loan information with each major bureau can be expensive. As a result, smaller lenders sometimes avoid these expenses and report to only one bureau, or fail to report at all. We may be surprised when we review our credit report to find a lender who failed to report our loan to all three credit bureaus. It can become a huge issue when we are trying to build all three scores.

What good is a loan when trying to build a credit file and the lender does not report the loan information to the credit bureaus? Nothing. If a lender's account with a quality rating is not reported, the credit scores may lack sufficient information to correctly provide our true credit rating. Depending on our credit history, this lack of communication may truly affect our credit scores.

Before making application, we should first ask each lender if they report to all three major credit bureaus. No one should be embarrassed or feel that they are being too intrusive. These are our credit scores! For those of us trying to develop a credit history, the answer could possibly force us to look for another lender.

For current accounts, we should look for any unreported, quality loans in the credit file. A credit report identifies the credit bureaus reporting the loan information by displaying the acronyms (*XPN / Experian, EQX / Equifax*, and *TU / Trans Union*) adjacent to the account. If an unreported loan is discovered and needed to develop our scores, we should contact the lender for answers. If that lender refuses to report to all three bureaus, we may have to find a different lender to build scores.

Unreported loan information to all three credit bureaus is a common problem. It is better that we recognize the limitations of a lender before we take out a loan instead of after the loan is paid off. We should only use the services of those lenders who report to each bureau when we are building our credit scores.

7. Cosigner

Develop credit through a cosigner

One option available to us when building credit references is to utilize the services of a cosigner. A cosigner is one way for those of us with lower or no scores to develop quality credit. Using a person who has a high credit score as a cosigner can help us establish quality credit references so that we can build a score.

A cosigner allows a person to develop a credit in a new credit file, or to rebuild a credit history following past financial challenges. A cosigner is used in conjunction with auto or personal loans, mortgages, or other installment loans. There is a definite end to the cosigned loan when the loan is paid off.

Each loan application process view cosigners in different ways. All parties must usually complete the loan application, have credit checked and income verified. Auto and personal loans generally use the higher of the two credit scores from either the main borrower or the cosigner. A mortgage usually uses the lower of the scores from the parties involved.

Once the loan is approved, all parties subsequently sign the loan documents and are obligated to repay the loan. The payment history is usually reflected on each individual's credit file. If any payments are made late, they are reflected in everyone's credit file and all scores are affected. Once the loan is paid off and closed or refinanced, the cosigner has no future obligation to the loan.

If the loan is still outstanding and the cosigner wants to remove his responsibility, the loan must usually be refinanced. Otherwise, the cosigner could be responsible for payments until the loan is paid off — which could be up to 30 years for a mortgage.

Before using a cosigner, we should have an exit strategy after our credit scores are sufficiently high enough to take sole responsibility for the loan. This strategy should allow the cosigner at some forward time to have the borrower refinance and remove the cosigner's name from the loan. In order to make cosigning an effective tool to raise credit scores, the parties should identify a quality lender who reports to all three major credit bureaus. If a cosigner is used and the payment information is not reported to each bureau, the value of the cosigner is limited. When loan information is properly reported, the main borrower is more likely to obtain future loans without the services of a cosigner.

8. Authorized-User Accounts

One little known method to build a credit score

Ever wanted to have another person's loan placed into our credit file in order to establish some credit? A little known method to develop credit is the use of an authorized-user account. Authorized-user accounts allow one party access to another person's revolving line of credit. This approach can quickly raise scores within a short period of time.

The parties involved are usually family members or close friends. With the lender's permission, a person is added to the account and the loan information can then be transmitted to both borrower's credit files. The account information and its payment history are recorded and a credit reference is established. We should check with the lender before adding someone to an account to make sure such an individual can receive credit for the account.

Most authorized-user accounts are used in conjunction with revolving lines of credit such as bank or retail credit cards. They can remain open for years and provide an instant and valuable reference to those building or re-establishing credit. Such loans can produce a quality reference if timely monthly payments are made and balances are kept low. Allowing access to a person's credit line through an authorized-user account is one great method to develop another person's credit file and credit.

There are some important details, however, to understand before signing off on this transaction. Since this loan can be reported to both party's credit file, the monthly payments will count against everyone on the loan. If late payments are made, they will also reflect negatively in both credit reports. Since billing statements are usually sent to the primary borrower, the authorized-user may never learn that loan payments are behind until it is too late to remedy the problem. Any late payments, debt, and monthly payments may affect our ability to qualify for future loans. Finally, if we want to be removed from the loan, we may have difficulty deleting the account and its balance from our credit report.

There is one additional note of caution. Several questionable entities have been selling quality loan references to those with lower scores. These companies charge thousands of dollars to put one valuable credit reference on an individual's credit report in hopes of raising a score. Because of these dubious practices, credit agencies or lenders could place additional restrictions on authorized-user accounts. What has been a valuable tool to establish credit for some, could face additional restrictions, or, in due course, be taken away.

9. Secured Loans

Use banking institutions to establish credit

One of the greatest sources for establishing credit is with a bank, credit union, or savings and loan center. Even if we have no access to a cosigner or an authorized-user account, we can still establish a credit history by opening a loan using a saving's account as security. This loan helps a person with limited, bad, or no credit from secured funds in a savings account at the bank.

Many of us have established our first loan with a cosigner, through an authorized-user account, or with a pre-approved credit card. Secured savings loans are for those of us who do not have any of these options available. Many smaller banks, credit unions, and savings and loan centers offer secured revolving lines of credit to help us develop credit and create future business opportunities. Once we have developed a relationship with that financial institution, we generally use them for checking accounts and future loans.

While applying for a credit line, we may be asked if we can provide some collateral for the credit. The collateral for this loan usually comes in the form of a savings account. We must then provide collateral in a savings account with the depository institution before the line of credit is approved. This line of credit usually starts out small such as a few hundred dollars.

For example, a person may be asked by the lender to provide a $500 cash savings account for a $500 line of credit on a credit card. The savings cannot be removed while the loan is still open. Once the line is closed and satisfactorily paid off and closed, the savings can be returned to the borrower. This is called a *'secured loan'*.

The payment history on the secured loan is reported to the credit bureaus and a credit rating is established. Hopefully, the lender reports to all three credit bureaus so that a good credit reference is established with each credit file. After six to twelve months, a respectable credit rating can be generated and scores can be created.

A quality credit score can be established even after one quality payment history reference. We can then apply for additional credit and receive loan approval without being required to provide additional collateral. The lines of available credit may increase as the credit scores improve. Loans secured with savings provide us an opportunity to build quality credit scores when no other opportunities are available.

10. Opportunities

Utilize personal relationships to develop credit

Even when we have no cosigner or savings for collateral, we still have other possibilities to develop our credit rating. Other opportunities may open up to us if we will only realize what is available. Such opportunities include current business relationships at the local bank, pre-approved credit offers, or those credit card companies that visit university campuses.

One potential possibility to establish credit is with our local bank or credit union where we already have our checking and savings accounts. Many of us have been approved for our first credit card from our primary bank because of an established relationship with our family. There could be similar opportunities from the local bank or credit union for most everyone who is trying to establish credit.

Smaller community banks generally try harder to develop customer relationships than their larger counterparts. They have a greater desire to expand their customer base and develop new business relationships at a personal level. We can meet face to face with the loan officer who reviews our application. Bigger banks are less personal since most of their lending decisions are through computer systems or over the telephone. The only real concern with smaller banks is that they may not report to all three credit bureaus.

Another possible option to establish credit is for students going to college. Many major national credit card companies and banks visit campuses to establish accounts with new clients. They want to develop long-term relationships with college students because of their income potential. They understand that students usually have limited income while attending college. However, they are working with students whose potential income should increase dramatically after college. Even though there is some risk for lenders, there is a potential relationship that can flourish for years to come.

Whatever our challenges may be, there should be many possibilities for us to develop our credit rating. All it really takes to develop our credit scores is one loan with on-time payments and some responsibility. After a short period of time, other options may soon arrive at the door. We just need to take some time and look around at all our options.

11. Utilities

◆───◆

Some utility companies report to the credit bureaus

One last avenue we may have to develop our credit history is from utility companies. Many of the bigger utility companies that offer cable, telephone, gas, and electric are now reporting to at least one of the three major credit bureaus. This change allows those of us without any established credit to build our credit file using unconventional means.

Utility companies have practically never reported their payment information to the credit agencies until recently. There were so many credit agencies, utilities would have had to report several times over to each bureau making the cost excessively high. There was no real benefit for utility companies to report because the cost was more than the benefit.

That policy is quickly changing. Recently some of the bigger utility companies have started to report to at least one of the three major credit bureaus. In the next few years, we will see most, if not all, of the utility companies report their monthly payment history to at least one of the three major credit bureaus. It is one way they can better manage their accounts. If it affects our credit report, we will pay more attention to our utility bills and not let them skip a month or two.

For those of us building or rebuilding our credit, it can be a valuable source to establish our rating. We should check with each utility company to learn if they report to the credit bureaus on a regular basis. We may find that one of the utility companies for our cellular phone, home phone, electric, gas, or cable actually reports to the credit bureaus. If they do, we can establish at least one credit score through this account.

It may surprise some that our utility account information is being reported to the credit agencies. Many utility companies still do not report our payments to the credit bureaus. We must check with them when we open, or if we already have an account open. If they are reporting to the credit agencies, we must be attentive to our utility bills to make sure they are paid on time. Otherwise, we could hurt our credit rating.

6

Quality Credit

Jen, a single woman in her late twenties, had made a concerted effort for several years to develop a very attractive credit file. She had over 25 credit references without one blemish. However, she notice her credit score had dropped after closing several credit card accounts. She failed to realize that credit scores are greatly influenced by recent loan activity. If some longer established accounts are closed, this action can be detrimental to credit scores.

Jen elected to close all of her credit card accounts because she was not using them. She felt that she could apply and take out a new credit card at any moment. As previously noted, the Classic credit score model must have some recent credit activity to properly score. If there is no loan activity, credit scores can decline and even drop off entirely.

Jen realized this problem before it became a real issue. She immediately called back one of the credit card companies and re-opened the account. Even though she still had an auto loan and a mortgage, closing all of her credit cards negatively impacted her scores. Credit scores look for a mixture of credit activity including installment and revolving debt. Finding that proper level is important to increasing our scores.

Various loans and lenders provide different values to credit scores. Too little or too much, this lender versus that lender, can either positively or negatively impact our credit scores. Every loan brings some value. The question is: *How much value?* Some loans from a certain lender can negatively impact our scores for years even after the loan has been paid off. Limiting credit to one specific loan type can also hurt our scores while a variety of loans can raise them

There are several types of lenders that we can use to develop our credit file. Many of us are unaware that lenders are given different values by

Types of Loans

Lenders	Example
1. Real Estate	*Mortgage or home equity loan.*
2. Installment - Closed-end loans	*Auto loan, education loan, personal loan.*
3. Revolving - Open ended loans	*Credit cards, personal lines of credit, overdraft accounts.*
4. Other / Collection	*Collection companies or attornies.*

This list is provided to assist in recognizing the different type of loans.

the credit score models. There are five reason codes that reference specific lenders. Reason codes 3, 15 and 29 (see Addendum A) require that we have some revolving activity with a bank or national credit Card activity. Codes 4 and 23 mention that we can have too many accounts with such lenders. Reason code six is the only one that references a specific lender to avoid. Loans from banks and national credit card company have a higher value than a merchant lender or finance company.

There are 10 reason codes that reference the type of account. Codes 3, 4, 10, 11, 15, 16, 23, and 24 reference issues with revolving accounts while 32 and 33 reference certain requirements with installment loans. Reason code issues a vague warning requiring us to have either installment or revolving loan activity. We can have too little or too much with a specific type of account.

Finding the right lenders with the proper mix of installment and revolving loans is essential to achieve the greatest value with our credit score. Even with a quality payment history, failure to find that proper level limits our ability to improve them. Whether we want to establish new credit or have a seasoned record, identifying the right lenders with the right mix of loans is essential for us to achieve an 800 level credit score.

Once these acceptable levels of credit risk are understood, we can recognize the time element each individual factor impact our scores. Some of these factors can affect a score for several years while others can be eliminated within a few months. Those factors that we can correct immediately should be addressed first in order to more quickly raise a score in the short term. As we properly chart our course, we can reach the upper echelon of the credit scoring range.

12. Valuable Lenders

Use lenders who provide the greatest value

One feature of the credit scoring system that most consumers are un-aware is that some distinct lenders have greater value. Certain lenders are actually preferred since they can raise our scores while other lenders can negatively impact them. We must recognize those valuable lenders for our credit needs in order to raise our scores.

There are many types of lenders that loan money for mortgage, auto, consumer, and personal loans. Such lenders include banks, mortgage companies, national credit card companies, credit unions, retail lenders, finance companies, private lenders, and payday lenders.

"Too few bank revolving accounts" (3), *"Lack of recent bank revolving information"* (15), and *"No recent bank card balances"* (29), demonstrate the greater value of certain lenders. Banks bring a higher value to credit scores than most other installment and revolving account lenders.

As a general guideline, those lenders with tighter credit requirements provide more value to credit scores. Banks are highly regarded from credit scores because their credit qualifications for loans are usually more stringent than other lenders. They use our deposits from checking, savings, and certificate of deposits (CDs) for home equity, auto, personal and credit card loans. For that reason, banks are heavily regulated by federal and state regulators to protect our money from negligence. Consequently, regulators limit the ability of banks to lend to those with lower credit scores. As a note, credit unions are not considered banks and are regarded as less valuable lenders in the credit scoring system.

On the other end of the lending spectrum, we have finance companies. One loan with a finance company can substantially drop our score. *"Too many consumer finance accounts"* (6) gives us a warning sign when we have used this type of lender. Many finance companies are lenders used by auto dealerships and retail stores for their on-site financing. They also offer home equity, credit card, and personal loans.

We should identify and utilize those lenders such as banks for our credit needs. Auto loans, credit cards, and home equity loans should be taken out with these types of lenders. By using such quality creditors, we will see the added value to our scores over time.

13. Installment Loans

Have at least one installment loan

The complex credit models value a mixture of loans to drive our credit scores higher. A proper mixture of credit includes activity from an installment loan. Understanding and having the proper number of installment loans is important to continue our drive to 850.

An installment loan has consistent monthly payments over a predetermined set of time and is closed when the loan is paid off. This loan can have a fixed or variable interest rate. If the loan is a variable rate installment loan, the monthly payment is determined by the balance and the adjustable interest rate. A fixed rate installment loan on the other hand has monthly payments which are predetermined at the time the note is signed. Unlike revolving loans, the monthly payment on an installment loan remains the same until the loan is paid off, regardless of any extra principal payments made. Timely installment loan payments demonstrate that we can meet obligations consistently every month over a set period of time.

Installment loans have a definite conclusion or last payment at the end of term. The length of installment loan term is predetermined at the time the loan papers are signed. For example, a five year loan would generally require payments for sixty months with the last payment being due at the sixtieth month, unless the loan is paid off prior to the end of the term. Installment loans can come in the form of a mortgage, an education loan, an auto loan, or a personal loan. A mortgage can last up to 40 years, an education loan usually lasts up to ten years (depending on deferments), an auto and personal loan can be open up to six years.

"Too few accounts with recent payment information" (Code 31 EFX / XPN & Code 34 - TU), and *"Lack of recent installment loan information"* (Code 32 - EFX / XPN & Code 4 - TU), both highlight the value of having at least one active installment loan in our credit history. An installment loan can be open for 40 years or as little as one month. Having payment activity from at least one installment loan is required to meet the criteria. The amount owed is usually irrelevant; the type of loan is the important factor.

We can have only revolving accounts in our credit report without an installment loan. We will still have a credit score, but it's ability to increase will be limited over time. To maximize our scores, we should have at least one active installment loan.

14. Revolving Accounts

Maintain at least one open revolving account

People often pay off and close their credit card accounts because they think it hurts their credit rating. When we pay off credit cards, we often elect to close the account. If we close all the open lies of credit in out report, we can hurt our credit scores. We must maintain at least one revolving line of credit to increase our credit scores.

Unlike installment loans, revolving loans have payments that vary from month to month. These monthly payments are determined not only by the monthly interest rate, but more importantly by the outstanding balance. When the balance is higher, the monthly payment are higher. As balances are paid down, the monthly payment declines.

"Lack of recent revolving account information" (16) is the warning sign that appears when we fail to have at least one open revolving account. With the *Classic* credit score model, the lack of recent open revolving account in the last six months can raise this level of credit risk. When there are no open revolving lines of credit, the credit score models cannot properly evaluate a our ability to manage this type of credit, and the result is lower scores.

Revolving accounts can be opened for a home equity loan, credit card, merchant or department store account, personal line of credit, or an overdraft account. We must demonstrate an ability to manage credit over an extended period of time with revolving accounts. If we take out the entire available line, we can hurt credit scores by demonstrating a poor ability to manage credit. By maintaining low balances, we display greater responsibility.

To eliminate the risk from a lack of revolving loan history, we should have at least one open revolving account. Most lenders allow revolving accounts to stay open indefinitely if we periodically use them. They can provide an added depth for years and even decades that we cannot find with installment loans. We do not always have to necessarily carry balances with our revolving accounts. Rather, we should open and use them occasionally. They can provide great depth for a credit score.

If we have just one open revolving loan account, we must make certain that that lender reports to all three credit bureaus. Otherwise, we could fail to build all three credit scores if our only open revolving account is only reporting to one of the three major credit bureaus.

15. Banks and Credit Card Companies

One open bank revolving or national credit card account

In the introduction to this chapter, we highlighted the need to identify those valued lenders. Revolving loans from banking institutions or national credit card companies add a certain value to credit scores that cannot be found with other lenders. Unless there is an open and active revolving loan with one of these companies, a certain risk factor may appear as a determining issue impacting our scores.

Banks have a higher value to our scores because of their stringent credit requirements. The credit score models also give similar value to national credit card companies such as *American Express*, *Capital One*, and *Discover*. *"Too few bank revolving accounts"* (3), appears when we fail to have a revolving loan with one of these lenders.

This factor requires that we have at least one open revolving account from a banking institution or national credit card company. If we have no open accounts with a banking institution or all our open credit cards are with credit unions or merchants accounts, we can drop our scores.

We can meet this requirement by simply having an over-daft account with our personal checking account at a bank. We may also open a home equity loan, credit card, or personal line of credit from the bank. The bank can be a federal or state bank. Most banks use *'Bank'* as part of their official name. If there is a question, we can locate federal banks at the following website:

www.federalreserve.gov/releases/lbr/
www.federalreserve/releases/mob/

If we don't use a bank for our checking and savings accounts or loans, we can still meet the criteria if we establish a credit card with a national credit card company. It just takes one revolving account with one of these lenders to meet the demands of the credit score models.

Last of all, we need to periodically use at least one bank or national credit card account. *"No recent bank card balances"* (29) requires that we use this account. If we only use our department store accounts for example, we can still hurt our scores. If we elect to only use one revolving account, it is best that it be from a bank or national credit card account since we can satisfy this stipulation, and *"No recent revolving balances"* (24) from this one credit line.

16. Merchant Accounts

◆━━━━━━━━━━━━━━━━━━━━━━━━━━━━━◆

They tie your purchase with financial services

When we make a purchase, we are regularly asked, *"Do you want to open an ABC account and save 10% on this purchase?"* We have all been bombarded with these offers. If we stop and elect to finance the purchase on a 10% discount and take out a 90, 180, or 360 days same-as-cash option or receive a free gift, we can actually hurt our scores in the coming months and years.

Customer service representatives are actually given all types of awards for persuading us to apply for an in-house store account. The more applications for credit, the more financial rewards are given to the salesman. Why are merchants so interested in our financing? They make more money on us. Even though they may have attractive incentives, they can actually negatively impact our scores.

Department stores and many other retail stores have their own financing in-house or have contractual arrangements with a lender who finances their customer's needs. If someone does not have the money to purchase the item, retailers can then make more money by offering financing options. Retailers make money both on the purchase and the financing. We are then more likely to return to the store to purchase additional items over the coming months and years.

When we open several retail store accounts to save some money, we can actually raise a couple of concerns with our scores. *"Too many accounts recently opened"* (9) is the warning sign when we have recently opened too many accounts. Even one new account can negatively impact our scores. *"Number of established accounts"* (28) also appears as a warning sign when we have too many open accounts. With or without balances, this matter can drop our scores.

Many of us forget about these accounts and they can remain open for years with no activity or oversight. These merchants want to keep these accounts open because they hope we will return to shop again with them. They can be very difficult to close. We should not open every new merchant account offer with its accompanying inquiry and recent new loan on our credit. We should be careful and only chose those accounts that we know we will use over time and are financed directly with the retail outlet. If it is a one-time purchase, we should look elsewhere for financing since the damage to our score can be substantial and impact our scores for the next couple of years. By being aware, we can avoid these pitfalls that can actually drop our credit scores.

17. High Risk Lenders

Avoid lenders that raise our levels of credit risk

Many consumers are unaware that there are lenders that can actually *hurt* our credit score. On the other end of the spectrum from banks are finance companies and pay day lenders who offer fast cash in return for higher rates. Their rate of default is also higher from a lack of tighter credit qualifications. Since they generally lend to those with less qualified credit, the credit scoring models give them very limited value.

Finance companies are privately funded lenders that do not have deposits to help fund loans. Since finance companies usually have higher cost of funds than savings and certificates of deposits, they charge considerable higher rates than banks. Even more confusing, many finance companies are owned by banks. However, finance companies do not have federal and state bank regulators reviewing their credit decision on loans. To identify them, they have their own designation by the credit bureaus and usually include, *'Finance'* or *'Financial'* as part of their name. In the financial world, they are called, *'Easy money lenders.'*

These companies often finance many merchant, department store, and auto dealerships loans. They also offer financial services to many retail stores to promote business. In return, these stores can offer 90 days, six months, and 12 months same-as-cash offers. They also solicit mortgages, auto, personal, and lines of credit to their current client base who may need money fast. Even if we elect to take out a short-term loan to finance a purchase, finance companies can actually damage our score for years after the loan has been paid off.

Pay day lenders are also utilized for quick cash needs. They charge higher fees and their interest rates are always exceedingly high. We can take out a loan in a matter of minutes instead of the longer process with banks. Since they are generally small in size, they may not report to the credit bureaus unless the account goes to collection.

"Too many consumer finance companies" (6) tells us to avoid these high risk lenders. According to *Fair Isaac*, the *Classic* scoring model is more punitive on credit scores than the *NextGen* model. The strategy should be the same. When we discover an open finance company loan, we should pay off and close the account as soon as possible. One loan is too many. The best solution is to identify and never take out a loan with finance companies. To identify them, we should ask the lender (some do not readily admit it) if they take deposits for savings accounts. If they do not, chances are they are a finance company.

Revolving Accounts

For most of us, revolving accounts make up most of open accounts in our credit file in the form of credit cards, department store accounts, or other lines of credit. Our ability to properly manage these revolving accounts is critical to increasing our credit score. Recognizing certain critical levels for these accounts has a major influence on our ability to raise our credit score over the years.

Many of us establish our first account reference in our credit file when we are approved and open our first credit card. These first revolving accounts can go along way in determining our future credit score. We can be irresponsible and abuse these accounts which can lead to many years of a depressed credit score, or we can be responsible and these accounts can drive our scores higher. There are several issues with our revolving accounts that are important factors for a higher score.

Jack and Glenda had been married almost 40 years. They had established multiple credit accounts right after they were married. In 2006, they had a Sears credit account that had been opened over 35 years and two other accounts that had been opened over 20 years.

Glenda heard that they should close all unused accounts to drive their credit score higher. They closed these three accounts because they had not used them for many years. They only kept those accounts open that they were currently using.

After a few months, they were perplexed that their score had dropped over 30 points. They were expecting their scores to increase because they had closed several unused credit card accounts. They later learned that the length of time their active credit card accounts are opened is a factor in their credit scores. Unlike installment loans, most revolving accounts can remain open for years and even decades if we only peri-

odically use them. With Jack and Glenda, all their current active credit cards were now only open less than six years which was now less valuable to their credit scores. Misinformation had cost them a substantial decline in their scores.

With revolving accounts, we must not only be attentive to the length of time they are open, we must also pay particular attention to the number of revolving accounts open, the number of bank or national credit card accounts open, the number of revolving accounts with balances, the individual debt ratios, the balances, the credit limits, and the account activity. Failure to recognize each issue and properly manage our revolving accounts are common mistakes we can continually make that hurt our scores.

We, as consumers, tend to have a credit card account or other line of credit outside acceptable ranges for the credit score system. Three common factors that hurt credit scores are *"Proportion of balances to credit limits too high on revolving accounts"* (10), *"Too many accounts with balances"* (5) and *"Length of time revolving accounts have been established"* (12). We should review each revolving account in our credit file ('Rev' under loan type or a line of credit on a residential property) to make sure that we are within acceptable ranges. If we are not within those acceptable levels, we need to make adjustments with our revolving accounts.

18. Revolving Account Balances

◆━━━━━━━━━━━━━━━━━━━━━━━━━━━━━━━━━━━◆

Maintain some activity with revolving loans

We may reach a certain point when we have one or two open lines of credit, but we fail to build our score. We may be financially set or have no need to borrow money. Simply leaving revolving accounts open without any recent activity may be insufficient to increase our score. The use of at least one revolving account (preferably a bank or national credit card) helps increase our credit scores.

There are five factors that can be impacted from a lack of revolving account activity. *"Lack of recent revolving account information"* (16) can become an issue when we have no open revolving accounts in our credit history. *"No recent revolving balances"* (24) goes one step further when we have no recent borrowing activity from at least one revolving account.

Additionally, *"Too few bank revolving accounts"* (3) appears when we have no open revolving accounts with a bank or national credit card company. *"No recent bankcard balances"* (29) becomes an additional factor when we fail to use a credit card or another revolving line of credit in the last six to twelve months from a bank or national credit card company. We may have an account open, but we have not recently used it. The credit report identifies the last time an amount was borrowed on the line of credit by the *'Last active date'*. Finally, *"Lack of recent revolving history"* (15) can warn us after we had at least one open revolving account with a bank or national credit card company, but we closed all of them and there has been no recent activity.

As previously commented, establishing a line of credit shows a certain responsibility. However, using these particular lenders for our accounts demonstrates an even greater responsibility. Credit scores not only look at active revolving loans, they also look at a our ongoing ability to borrow and make timely payments on the loan.

The best way to avoid all these issues is to have at least one open bank or national credit card revolving account and use it periodically. If we fail to do so, we may jeopardize a stellar credit rating. Creditors may will close our lines of credit even after a year of inactivity. Other creditors may wait for up to three years or longer before they close any unused accounts. We need to use at least one revolving line of credit, preferably from a bank or from a national credit card company. Even a small balance on a revolving account is sufficient to meet this credit score requirement.

19. Golden Accounts

Identify those established accounts and keep them open

As highlighted in the chapter heading, too many people have been told to close their older unused revolving accounts. That can be true — if we have an excessive number of open accounts. However, numerous people have closed their older more established accounts because of their lack of use. This has led to a decline in their credit scores since the older more established accounts are no longer open.

Most revolving accounts or personal lines of credit can remain open indefinitely, as long as the accounts are used periodically. These accounts can be *'golden'* credit references if timely payments are made and low balances are maintained. *"Length of time revolving accounts have been established"* (12) identifies the length of time all credit card and other personal lines of credit have been open.

We may be surprised and unaware of all of our revolving accounts still open. Upon review of our credit report, we may find older department store accounts still open from years ago. National credit card companies and department store accounts are known to leave their accounts open for years, even if we don't use them. They want us to return to use their services at some future point in time. These accounts may be our longest active revolving accounts. We should not close them. Revolving accounts such as bank or department store credit cards can have a life of their own. They can go on for 30, 40, and even 50 years or more. Home equity loans tend to have 10, 20, or a maximum 30 year term.

The difference in an 700 credit score and a 800 credit score can often be attributed to the length of time we have our revolving accounts open. Those of us who have the majority of our revolving accounts open for more than seven years, the greater the chance of credit scores in the 800s. Closing an older account because it has a higher interest rate may be a mistake. We should recognize its value to our score before we close it. Those revolving accounts that are over ten years old should practically never be closed. They are considered, *'Golden accounts'*. One of our best strategies with our credit scores is to establish between two to four *'Golden accounts'* in our credit report. They have a multiple positive effects on our scores.

If we have too many open revolving accounts in a well established credit file, we should close those that have been opened the shortest period of time (and have at least one bank or national credit card account remain open) to avoid a decline in our credit scores.

20. Credit Card Balances

Reduce balances on credit card accounts

There are six methods by which the credit scoring system measures the amount of debt we have. The first measurement addresses the balances on unsecured revolving lines of credit such as credit cards and overdraft accounts. (The remaining five are found on pages 54 (2), 60, 65, & 80) We may have credit cards that carry a balance every month. In other instances, we may payoff our credit card debt every billing cycle. The higher the balances on these accounts, the lower our credit scores.

"Amount owed on revolving accounts is too high" (11) factors into our scores when we have at least one credit card or unsecure line of credit that has an excessively high balance. The impact can be felt from a bank, department store, or national credit card account. It has no preference. This issue is more apparent with scores in the 700 to 800 range and at least one credit card balance over $8,000.

There are two credit cards from the same lender, both having a $20,000 credit limit and opened the same length of time. One has a balance of $10,000 and the second has balance of $2,000. The account with the $10,000 balance would have a substantial negative effect on our scores.

If we carry balances on our credit cards or personal line of credits, what is the maximum balance we should have on these accounts for an 800 credit score? We should maintain balances below $3,000 for each credit card and other unsecured revolving account. We can drop our balances even more. The lower the reported balances, the higher the credit score.

If this factor is affecting our scores, we should reduce that credit card debt by paying down the balance, or consolidating such debt into one non-credit card account such as a home equity loan.

Credit Report

Companies	Credit Limit	Balance	Type
CED Home Equity	$50,000	$12,000	Rev
XYZ Credit Card	$15,000	$10,100	Rev
HIJ Line of Credit	$3,500	$450	Rev
WXY Credit Card	$1,000	$275	Rev

The concern is with the XYZ account because the balance is excessively high.

21. Debt Ratios

Maintain debt ratios below 50% of their high credit limits

The second measurement of debt used by the credit scoring system is the debt ratio. Most people have never heard of a debt ratio. If they have, they think it is the figure used to qualify for a loan. The debt ratio is one of the most problematic issues for many consumers' credit scores. When we increase our balances on revolving accounts in relation to their high credit limits, our credit risk grows and our scores decline. Keeping the debt ratio low on each revolving account is extremely important if we want to have excellent credit scores.

This ratio is determined by dividing the balance on each revolving account into its respective high credit limit. This calculation reveals the balance to high credit limit ratio or *'Debt Ratio.'* When we have high debt ratios, we fail to demonstrate responsibility with our revolving accounts. *"Proportion of balances to high credit limit too high on revolving accounts"* (10) appears when we have even one account with a high debt ratio. The higher the debt ratio and the greater number of revolving accounts with high debt ratios, the greater the decline in scores. If we have multiple high debt ratios, we may also see, *"Amount owed on accounts is too high"* (1) which is the third measurement of debt. This ratio does not factor into installment and some mortgage loans. Those are determined by the loan balance ratio and they are discussed later.

To calculate our debt ratios, we must first review all our open revolving accounts with balances. This can include all credit cards, merchant accounts, personal lines of credit (usually appear as 'REV' under loan type) and home equity loans (show up as 'MTG' or mortgage under loan type). If a home equity loan is set up as a line of credit, it is usually considered a revolving account. We should calculate each debt ratio on every open revolving account in our credit report. Any debt ratio on just one account exceeding 50% can cause a serious drop to our scores.

There are two credit cards with credit limits of $3,000 each. Credit card A has a balance of $2,500 and credit card B has a balance of $500. Credit card A will drop credit scores because of its high debt ratio at 83%. Credit card B has no real effect on scores from its 20% debt ratio.

If we have multiple revolving accounts with debt ratios between 80 and 110% of our credit limits, our scores are probably in the 500 to 600 range. If all our debt ratios are between 20 and 50% , we are usually in the 700s. If our ratios are below 20%, our scores are usually in the 800s. Lower debt ratios on revolving accounts lead to higher credit scores.

Debt Ratios

There are three examples provided of how high debt ratios impact credit scores. The first example has every debt ratio below 50% and even a few below 20%. The second example has just one account with a high debt ratio. Its impact can be apparent when we drop the balance below 50% on that one account. The third example has multiple revolving accounts with debt ratios above 50% and even one above 100%. It's impact on scores is substantial. The difference between examples one and three can be over 100 points.

Example #1

Companies	Credit Limit	Balance	Debt Ratio	Type
CED Home Equity	$40,000	$8,000	20%	Mtg
XYZ Credit Card	$2,500	$1,000	40%	Rev
HIJ Line of Credit	$1,500	$150	10%	Rev
WXY Credit Card	$1,000	$120	12%	Rev

There is no real concern with any of these revolving accounts.

Example #2

Companies	Credit Limit	Balance	Debt Ratio	Type
CED Home Equity	$40,000	$8,000	20%	Mtg / Rev
XYZ Credit Card	$2,500	$1,550	62%	Rev
HIJ Line of Credit	$1,500	$150	10%	Rev
WXY Credit Card	$1,000	$120	12%	Rev

The concern is the XYZ credit card because ratio is high..

Example #3

Companies	Credit Limit	Balance	Debt Ratio	Type
CED Home Equity	$40,000	$28,000	70%	Mtg / Rev
XYZ Credit Card	$2,500	$2,550	102%	Rev
HIJ Line of Credit	$1,500	$1000	67%	Rev
WXY Credit Card	$1,000	$950	95%	Rev

All of them are a huge concern to credit scores. One revolving account is over 100%, a second is over 80% with the other two over 50%.

22. High Debt Ratios

Recognize available strategies to lower high debt ratios

Once we are aware of the debt ratio, we need to always keep balances below 50% of the high credit limit. When we have high debt ratios on credit cards, home equity loans, or revolving credit lines, they can lower our scores for years until we resolve the problem. When we have at least one revolving account with a high balance ratio, we should look at some possible strategies to limit its negative impact on our scores.

Each person's financial and credit situation is different. What loans we take out, how much we borrow, and pay back is always different. Nevertheless, this issue, outside of late payments, affects more scores than any other factor. We should avoid borrowing too much from our revolving accounts in the first place. If we simply plan better, we hopefully can avoid this problem.

Oftentimes, we carry our entire credit card debt on one credit card or other personal line of credit that has the lowest interest rate. However, such accounts can cause substantial downward pressure on our scores. If we have a high balance ratio on at least one account, we can work a couple of strategies to drop this ratio. If we have the financial resources, we can simply pay down the debt. If we don't have the money, we can transfer all or part of the balance to another revolving account that has more available credit and little or no debt.

If we lack the resources to immediately pay down balances or make other adjustments, we can work to pay down the balances over time. It takes a lot of discipline. We should make extra payments and not charge on those accounts until we bring the debt ratio in line. If we currently have high ratios on several revolving accounts, we should first work to bring all of the debt ratios below 80%. Once accomplished, we should next work to ratios below 50%. Finally, as we work towards an 800 level credit score, we should finally drop this ratio on all credit cards, home equity loans, and other lines of credit below 20%. As we work our balances lower on our revolving lines of credit, our credit scores will increase. It is definitely worth the effort.

If we use a revolving line of credit, we should never let the account balance go above 50% of its high credit limit. The debt ratio needs constant monitoring on each revolving account. If we need to borrow a substantial amount of money, we should look at other possibilities first. Otherwise, it could drop our scores for months and years to come.

Strategies for High Debt Ratios

There are three examples of ways to reduce the debt ratios on revolving accounts. We can make adjustments with our accounts balances to reduce this issue's impact on our credit score.

Example #1

Companies	Credit Limit	Balance	Debt Ratio	Type
Before				
XYZ Credit Card	$1,500	$1,000	67%	Rev
HIJ Line of Credit	$1,500	$1,200	80%	Rev
After				
XYZ Credit Card	$1,500	$700	47%	Rev
HIJ Line of Credit	$1,500	$600	40%	Rev

Both revolving accounts have high debt ratios. The XYZ credit card is paid down $300, and the HIJ credit line is paid down $600. After both accounts are paid down, the debt ratios on both accounts are within acceptable ranges.

Example #2

Companies	Credit Limit	Balance	Debt Ratio	Type
Before				
XYZ Credit Card	$500	$400	80%	Rev
HIJ Line of Credit	$1,500	$0	0%	Rev
After				
XYZ Credit Card	$500	$0	0%	Rev
HIJ Line of Credit	$1,500	$400	27%	Rev

The XYZ credit card has a high debt ratio because of a lower credit limit. The balance is transferred to HIJ personal line of credit which has a higher limit.

Example #3

Companies	Credit Limit	Balance	Debt Ratio	Type
Before				
XYZ Credit Card	$1,500	$1,000	67%	Rev
HIJ Line of Credit	$1,500	$0	0%	Rev
After				
XYZ Credit Card	$1,500	$500	33%	Rev
HIJ Line of Credit	$1,500	$500	33%	Rev

The XYZ credit card has a high debt ratio. Part of the balance is transferred to HIJ personal line of credit to offset the high debt ratio on the HIJ credit card. This has dropped the debt ratio on the HIJ credit card while using the credit limit of another revolving account. When doing this strategy, we are establishing a balance on another account which can offset the increase in the score.

23. High Credit Limits

Raise credit limits to lower ratios

We sometimes elect to close our credit cards or personal lines of credit when they have excessively high credit limits. Other times, we may reduce the credit limits on these accounts thinking that either of these actions will benefit our credit scores. Either way, closing these accounts or reducing their limits can actually drop our scores. We should understand its implications before taking such action.

When we use these revolving lines of credit, the lower the debt ratio, the greater the value to scores. We demonstrate that we can manage credit extremely well. For example, we have two credit cards. Both accounts have balances of $2,000. One account has a $10,000 credit limit with a 20% ratio, while the $3,000 credit limit has a 67% ratio. We can reduce the impact on credit scores from *"Proportion of balances to credit limits too high on revolving accounts"* (10) when we raise our credit limits on our revolving accounts. We should try to raise them up as high as possible.

There is one word of caution. Raising up our credit limits can also lead to misuse. Raising limits is an effective way to increase credit scores, but can be a quick way to drop credit scores. If we need to borrow a substantial amount on a revolving account, we should ask the lender for the limit increase before raising the balance on the loan. If we wait until the debt ratio is over 50%, the high ratio may have already affected our scores, diminishing the chances for lender approval.

A higher credit limit on a credit card or other line of credit is a sign of responsibility. When credit card limits are $10,000 or more, they are especially valuable. Even a higher credit limit on a home equity loan can result in lower interest rates and greater value. Raising credit limits is one of the greatest strategies that can help us now for years to come.

Credit Report

Companies	Credit Limit	Balance	Debt Ratio
Account 1			
DEF Credit Card	$3000	$2000	67%
Account 2			
HIK Credit Card	$10,000	$2000	20%

The debt ratio is high. By raising the credit limit, it is reduced to 20%.

24. Closing Revolving Accounts

Pay off the entire balance before closing the account

We all periodically close a revolving account when we become dissatisfied with customer service, terms, interest rate, or there is no need for the account. Before closing the line of credit, we should pay off the entire account. Closing an account too early with an outstanding balance can possibly hurt our credit scores.

A debtor and a creditor both have the option to close a revolving credit line. When either party closes a revolving loan, we can no longer access its line of credit. If we ever want to reopen the line of credit, we must usually go through the lender's approval process again.

A revolving loan may be closed and still have an outstanding balance. The concern arises if the creditor elects to drop the high credit limit to $0. With this scenario, the credit scores could be negatively impacted since the balance is exceeding the high credit limit. We then appear to have borrowed more than the high credit limit. This situation creates a high balance ratio which can trigger the warning sign, *"Proportion of balances to credit limits is too high on revolving accounts"* (10).

In the given example, the borrower has a debt to credit limit of 40%. After the line is closed, the lender drops the credit limit to $0. The account is then $400 over the credit limit. The level of credit risk would then increase since there is a high debt ratio.

This potential issue only applies to revolving accounts. Before closing a revolving account, we should pay off the entire balance to make sure that the creditor does not drop the high credit limit to $0 with a balance remaining. We can then be assured that our credit scores are not negatively affected when we close a revolving account.

Credit Report

Companies	Credit Limit	Balance	Debt Ratio
Account 1			
DEF Credit Card	$1000	$400	40%
Account 2			
HIK Credit Card	$0	$400	400 over limit

If the credit limit is not reported, it can make it look like we are overextended.

25. Bank Revolving Accounts

Limit the number of open accounts

A certain amount of revolving loan activity is required to advance credit scores. As long as there is at least one bank revolving account open with some activity, our scores will respond positively for years. However, when we have an excessive number of open accounts, with or without balances, it can negatively impact our scores.

We may have an overdraft for our checking account, a credit card, a personal line of credit and a home equity loan all from our bank. It doesn't take long and we can have multiple accounts. If we have separate checking or savings accounts at multiple banks, we can really add up the number of revolving lines of credit.

"Too many bank or national revolving accounts" (4) may appear when we have an excessive number of credit cards, personal lines of credit, home equity loans or other revolving loans *with or without* balances. What is the correct number of revolving accounts we should have for an 800 credit score? We should have no more than three open revolving accounts from banks or national credit card companies. This figure excludes department store or merchant lenders.

When we review our credit report, almost all of us have at least one or two older revolving accounts we thought had been closed. Sometimes we find multiple accounts still open. When we select three accounts to keep open, we should identify revolving accounts that have been opened the longest and are without any delinquent payments.

There is one other potential concern to recognize. The fourth measurement of our debt load is the number of bank or national credit card companies with balances. *"Number of bank or national revolving accounts with balances"* (23) appears when we have an excessive number of revolving accounts **with balances from such institutions**. We should always keep the number of accounts **with balances** to a minimum no matter what type of lender or account. To keep this issue from dropping our scores, we should have no more than two revolving accounts **with balances** from banks or national credit card companies.

Number of accounts open and the number of accounts with balances can both impact our score. Keeping the number to a minimum can reduce our credit risk. Paying attention to all the different revolving accounts open and minimizing the number of accounts with balances can help us stay on the path to a reputable credit score.

26. New Accounts with Balances

Opening revolving accounts with a high balance

When we open a new credit card or home equity loan, we often take out most if not the entire credit line at the very beginning. When we pull out the entire credit line at the beginning, we can really drop our scores. This combination is a common mistake and adds great downward pressure on our scores when we purchase homes or consolidate debt.

The two credit risk factors involve, *"Too many accounts recently opened"* (9) and *"Proportion of balances to credit limits too high on revolving accounts"* (10). Such occurrences often happen when we purchase a new home or open a credit card account. Mortgage lenders utilize home equity loans to purchase a home. If we purchase a home and elect to put 5% down, the lender often has two mortgages to avoid mortgage insurance. The first mortgage has a loan-to-value of 80% and the second mortgage has a loan-to-value of 15% for a combined loan-to-value of 95%.

The second loan however is often a home equity loan or line of credit to keep the monthly payment low. Even though the line was used to purchase the house, its appears like we took out a line of credit and borrowed the entire amount. This scenario creates higher credit risk and lower credit scores. If a second mortgage is used, the home buyer should use a closed end or installment loan for the second mortgage.

With other situations, we may take out the entire amount on a credit card to consolidate debt or make a consumer purchase. We should only take out at a maximum up to 50% of the line whether it be a new credit card or home equity loan. For an 800 credit score, this is an especially important strategy especially for those loans less than 12 months old. Otherwise, the downward movement in our credit score can be quite substantial. The best strategy with new revolving accounts is to borrow the least amount against them for the first twelve months.

Payment History

Credit Report Date: 1/01/2007

Creditor	Opening Date	Limit	Balance	Type
FGD Mortgage	10/06	$240,000	$240,000	Mortgage
DCB Home Equity	10/06	$45,000	$45,000	Revolving

Two loans — one as a regular mortgage and a second as a home equity line. The second mortgage is impacting scores with a high debt ratio in addition to being a new account.

8

Installment Loans

In the credit score model, we are required to maintain at least one active installment loan. However, if we have too many opened loans, we can drop our scores from having too many loans with balances or by having high balances in relation to their initial loan limits. Too little, too much — *what is the correct level of installment loan debt?*

When we take out an installment loan, our loan balance is the initial loan amount or the figure in the credit report under the high credit limit. The debt ratio as measured on revolving accounts would be 100% on most installment loans. The credit scoring system gives us room to pay down our balances on installment loans. It recognizes that our loan balances are going to be high when we open a new installment loan.

Installment loans are open when they have a balance. Once the account has been paid off, the loan is closed. Common installment loans include a mortgage, auto, education, and personal loans. They have a set period of time open determined when the loan papers are signed.

Most installment loans pay down the balance over time. Some installment loans can have deferred payments such as education loans. There are some loans however that can actually increase in outstanding balance over time. These loans are called negative amortized loans. The payments on such loans fail to pay the accrued interest during a set period and the result can be an increasing loan balance above the initial loan amount. One such loan includes the recent popular Option Adjustable Rate Mortgage or Option ARM for home purchases. They actually can drop our credit scores if we let the balances increase.

Paying for school, buying a car, and finding a home are usually all challenges for those coming out of college. In a recent *Experian* study for

USA Today, the average level of installment loan debt in the form of education and auto loans has been rising over the last five years for those in the 20 to 29 age range. Education debt has increased an average 16% more in 2006 from 2001. Auto loan debt has increased a more modest 4%. This study shows the level of stress for those taking on new installment loan debt.

The question is, *"Can those starting out in life handle the payments on all this new installment loan debt?"* There are signs that are starting to give more indications of the problem. In the same *Experian* study, those in their twenties with a charge-off account rose to 49% from 43.8% just five years earlier. Not only are those in the 20 to 29 age range taking on new debt, more are falling behind on their payments drastically impacting their credit.

Many young college students go through college financing their education with student loans and credit card debt. They get out of college, find a job, buy a car, but they then have to start making payments on those education loans while looking for a new home. The challenges can be extreme.

We use installment loans to help us finance school, buy a particular car or home. However, they can also impact our credit scores if we take on too much debt at one time or fail to meet the monthly payments. Since installment loans usually have higher balances than their revolving counterparts, the payments are more challenging to meet.

We should be attentive to how they can impact our future scores when we take on such debt. Otherwise, we could take on new debt without a real plan to pay it back. That is a definite plan for disaster. For an 800 level credit score, we must reduce the number of installment loans.

27. Loan Balance Ratios

A lower ratio raises our scores

The fifth measurement of our debt load is the balances on our installment loans. We earlier reviewed the debt ratio with revolving accounts. The second critical ratio with our credit scores is the *'Loan balance ratio'*. The loan balance ratio does not have the same impact as the debt ratio. It's influence is less unless we take out multiple new mortgages, auto, and other installment loans within a short period of time.

The loan balance ratio is determined by dividing the outstanding balance on an installment loan into the initial loan amount. The initial loan amount is usually found under the high credit limit in the credit report. Unlike revolving lines of credit, the loan balance ratio is always 100% at the beginning for installment loans. A 100% debt ratio for revolving accounts would be extremely high and really drop our scores. The credit scoring system recognizes a revolving line of credit and an installment loan. Nevertheless, the lower the loan balance ratio, just like the debt ratio, the higher our credit scores when we pay down the balances on our mortgages, auto, education, and personal loans.

For example, we purchase a home for $300,000 and put down $100,000. Our initial loan amount and our loan balance are both the same at the beginning — $200,000. As we pay principal payments on the loan, the balance declines. If after three years we pay down $40,000 on our balance, our loan balance ratio would be 80% ($160,000 divided by $200,000). We reduce our credit risk when we can pay down the balances on our installment loans.

One high loan balance ratio is not going to have a substantive downward impact on our scores. The real risk from the loan balance ratio is when we open multiple installment loans especially mortgage or auto loans within a couple of years. If we pay regular monthly payments, our principal balances will take months and years to decline. We would be carrying multiple loans with high balances for several months and even years. Our credit scores would be negatively impacted from *"Loan amounts on installment loans is too high"* (3 TU, & 33 - EQX / XPN).

College students want to know the impact from multiple student loans. Students can carry high ratios on these loans for years until they finish school. For some, it could be six to eight years before payments start. Student loans carry great value for credit scores. Nevertheless, they are also subject to the loan balance ratio. The negative impact is minimal as long as both deferments and payments are made on time.

When we can have loan balances ratio less than 80%, we reduce our overall credit risk and we increase our scores. As we lower the loan balance ratio, the more valuable the loan is to our credit scores. We reflect more positively the faster and lower we drop our loan balances. As we space new installment loans and pay down the existing balances, these loans can become very valuable to our whole credit profile.

Loan Balance Ratios

There are two examples by which the loan balance ratios factor into our credit score. The first example has a negative impact, while example number two has a positive effect since balances have been paid down. The mortgages in these examples are fixed term (not revolving lines of credit).

Example #1

Companies	High Credit Limit	Balance	L.B. Ratio	Type
DCB Mortgage	$250,000	$248,000	99%	Mtg
JKL Mortgage	$155,000	$151,000	97%	Mtg
FGH Auto	$35,000	$33,000	94%	Ins
RST Auto	$23,000	$22,000	96%	Ins

All of them raise a concern since they are carrying balances that are close to the initial loan amounts (high credit limits). It appears that the borrower purchased two homes and two autos within a short period of time which would raise additional concerns of too many accounts recently opened. This would be determined by the opening dates on each account.

Example #2

Companies	High Credit Limit	Balance	L.B. Ratio	Type
DCB Mortgage	$250,000	$245,000	98%	Mtg
JKL Mortgage	$155,000	$75,000	48%	Mtg
FGH Auto	$35,000	$20,000	57%	Ins
RST Auto	$23,000	$10,000	43%	Ins

Even though the DCB Mortgage appears to be recently opened, the other three installment loans have balances that are paid down substantially below their initial loan amounts reducing the credit risk. This example highlights the need to space out new installment loans so that we don't create additional credit risk and drop our scores.

28. Loan Balances

Pay extra principal to lower loan balance ratio

An effective strategy that can payoff over time is to add extra principal payments on all of our installment loans. We should not only make our regular monthly payment with such loans, we should also add extra principal payments to pay down the balances faster and reduce our loan balance ratios on each installment loan.

As highlighted in the previous strategy, a considerable factor with our credit scores is the principal balance of each installment loan in relation to its initial loan balance. If our installment loan balances are close to the initial loan balances, we are adding risk. The battle with the loan balance ratio is how fast we can pay down our loan balances in comparison to their initial loan amounts. A good reference point is to lower that loan balance ratio on each installment loan to at least 80%.

We demonstrate greater responsibility when we pay down our balances on auto, mortgage, or educational loans. We reduce the effect from the issues of *"Amount owed on accounts is too high"* (1) or *"Proportion of loan balances to loan limits is too high"* (33 - EQU / XPN and 3 - TU) on our credit scores by paying extra principal payments. Such loans can fast become a tremendous asset by reducing our loan balances.

In order to reduce our balances, we should make an additional principal payment with each monthly payment. Even a small extra principal payment can make a difference. For example, if we have a 30 year $150,000 mortgage at 6.00%, our minimum monthly payment would be $899.33. After four years, our principal balance would be $141,732 if we did not add any extra principal payments. If we added an extra $100 with each monthly payment, our principal balance would drop to $136,195 after four years — an extra $5,537 in principal reduction.

That is almost a 4% extra decline in the principal balance and we would have saved $737 in interest over the first four years by adding that extra $100. These extra payments save thousands in interest and lower our balances at a faster rate in the years to come. The accounts become more valuable for a longer period of time.

Whether it is an auto, personal, or mortgage loan, we can impact our credit scores by adding extra to the principal balances. This fact can be a substantial difference maker with a credit score. Over the coming months and years, we can see our credit scores climb as we drive our principal loan balances lower.

29. Refinancing Loans

Refinancing or changing loans can impact scores

In the previous sections, we reviewed the strategy of lowering our balances from their initial loan amounts. One issue that can hurt our scores is refinancing an auto, mortgage, or education loan especially those that have been outstanding for several years. We can lose valued credit references if we have paid down the balance from the initial loan amount and then elect to refinance a loan. Refinancing an installment loan starts the process all over again.

We usually refinance installment loans for lower or fixed interest rates, or to consolidate balances. We may refinance mortgage, auto, education or personal loans that have had balances paid down. When we refinance such loans, we can lose that principal loan reduction so important to our scores. The loan balance is reset once again as the initial loan amount on the new loan. The more loans we refinance within a short period of time and the longer those loans have been outstanding, the greater the negative impact on our scores.

We take out a $200,000 mortgage. Our high credit limit shows $200,000 with a balance of $200,000. Within five years, we pay down the balance to $50,000 and our loan balance ratio is 75%. If we refinance that loan, the new loan reflects a high credit limit of $150,000 with a balance of $150,000. Our balance ratio just went from 75% back up to 100%. We have just lost a valuable reference to our scores.

We should always have a purpose when we refinance. Installment loans that have balances reduced by more than 20% from their initial loan amounts are valuable, as long as payments have been made on time and we have a quality lender. We should have a definite advantage from a lower interest rate, change to a higher quality lender (finance company to a bank), consolidate other loans, or payoff a delinquent account to offset the loss of that quality loan reference.

If we don't want to have a substantial negative impact on our scores, we should not refinance installment loans that have been outstanding for several years without a real purpose. The longer installment loans have been outstanding, the lower the principal balances and the loan balance ratios. If we must refinance an installment loan, we should expect some negative impact on our scores if we payoff an older more valuable installment loan that has a loan balance ratio below 80%.

9 Credit Management

Late one January night several years ago, a mortgage loan officer received a call at the office from an escrow officer at a local title company. "Jim, I need your help!" In the background, he could the sobs of a young lady. Something was horribly wrong. What this lady and her husband had discovered is that every 'free' incentive is not what it appears to be. There are always strings attached.

The escrow officer told the loan officer that she had a couple that was closing on their newly constructed home when things went bad. The couple was enticed by their builder to use his mortgage lender with $5,000 in so-called 'free' incentives. What the couple failed to realize is the extra costs in monthly payments and closing costs they must pay to receive those so-called 'free' incentives.

Nothing in life is for free. Home builders, like their auto salesmen counterparts, are savvy businessmen. They make offers appear, 'You can't pass this up!' In fact, they simply build the cost of the incentive into the sale of the house or car one way or another. Builders and auto dealers would be out of business if these incentives were truly free. They make a lot of money on us because of our lack of understanding.

The couple was supposed to have a $1,050 monthly payment with less than $1,000 to bring to the closing. When they arrived at their closing, they were shocked to find the monthly payment was almost $1,300 and they had to bring in $4,200. The wife just had given birth to twins a week prior to closing and the thought of having to pay a much higher monthly payment and come up with the extra closing costs was unreasonable. They simply could not afford the extra money for closing costs or the higher monthly payment. They were heading for a disaster that could cost them their home and their respective score for years to come.

The builder's loan officer was no where to be found. There was no where to turn and the couple knew they were over a barrel. This very scenario plays out time and time again everyday across America. We can get sucked into transactions that can cost us financially and impact our credit scores for years. We may think that we can get something for nothing. Fortunately, this couple backed away, postponed the movers, and took another two weeks to get another mortgage set up.

Salesmen, whether a builder, real estate agent, auto dealer, or any other salesman, not only want to sell us something, but also arrange our financing. In most every case, **Don't go down that road!** Transactions are setup to make them more money, not save us money. We can't receive something for nothing or those companies offering such incentives would soon be out of business.

We must always take control of every transaction to avoid conflicts of interest and to protect our financial stability and our credit scores. We should recognize these conflicts of interest that can easily turn into a nightmare. We can end up owing a lot more for the auto or home when using the *in-house* lender. It can truly jeopardize our credit scores as we end up over-paying for a major purchase.

Once the papers are signed, a mortgage or an auto loan can be extremely difficult to undo. We should all be cautious and not take the word of the salesman. These salesmen are just that, salesmen. They are out to sell something and a loan is often a part of their sales pitch. These loans can have a positive impact on credit scores or they can be extremely costly. We should use some caution so that we are not owing more than the value of our auto or our home.

We can get caught into bad loans because of extra incentives or the need to open a new loan. We may have multiple loans open with different creditors. What are the correct levels of debt? What is, *'too much'* that it can truly impact our credit scores? These are some of the questions for which we must determine the right answers.

There are many other strategies we can follow to protect and build a credit score. These strategies are very important if we want to build an 800 level credit score. We need to determine the correct levels of debt so that we can raise our credit scores.

30. A Reserve

Create a plan for needs and emergencies

We all face emergencies from time to time that can potentially cost us a lot of money and our credit rating. When we face such types of financial challenges, we often make poor decisions based upon immediate needs. By creating a reserve, we can better plan and protect our valued credit scores.

Unexpected auto or home repairs, medical bills, or other unforeseen expenses will come. We just don't know when or how much. Since many of us live from pay check to pay check, we face extreme pressures to meet these sudden expenditures since they come at the most inopportune times. We are subsequently more likely to make poor decisions when we have no plan. We may open a new account, be forced to take out a loan with a high risk lender, incur late payments, or even let bills go to collection. The problems can be never ending. A reserve is an important tool to improving and protecting our credit score.

Many problems with credit scores are created when we fail to have a substantive plan that can counter future emergencies. Problems can be alleviated with a short term financial reserve. To determine the amount of cushion, we should first identify our needs by reviewing our past. Individuals and families alike should develop a plan by reviewing the emergency expenses from the last year or two. We should try to have at least a three month reserve. Once we have determined a figure, we should set up a reserve from available resources.

We should first try to create a savings reserve to keep us out of debt. This is a preferred option. With some effort now during a more prosperous time, we may be able to establish a sufficient savings over a short period of time to counter many upcoming emergencies. If we are unable to establish a sufficient reserve from our savings, we should next look to a line of credit from a credit card or a home equity loan. The best time to establish a credit reserve account is when we don't need it.

Through a developed plan, we can take the sting from financial challenges in the future. Once the plan has been set, we should set guidelines when this reserve can be used. When emergencies occur, we can then utilize this savings or credit reserve and avoid making poor financial decisions that can create future emergencies and negatively impact our credit scores. Through better preparation, we can then develop some security and alleviate some of our credit risk.

31. Reporting Dates

Reporting dates are just as important as payment due dates

Opening dates, past due dates, last active dates, and reporting dates all have a substantial impact on our score. Most of us are concerned about making on-time payments by a given due date. However, reporting dates can have considerable influence on our credit scores. Since loan balances have a major impact on our credit score, we should know when our creditors report our account information to the credit agencies so that we can make our loan information look its best.

The process to create a credit score is similar to taking several individual pictures to create one big picture. When we have our picture taken, we like to dress in our best clothes, hair brushed, looking at the camera with a smile. With each of our accounts, lenders take an individual picture and send it to the credit agencies to compose the big picture. If one individual picture is missing, incorrect, or problematic, the big picture can show problems which can damage our score. Our credit score is based on that big picture. Hopefully, each individual picture reflects positively on us so our big picture looks its best and our scores increase.

The picture making or credit reporting takes time to process and send to each credit agency, where it eventually appears on our credit report. Our credit report at any given time is simply a composite of each individual account taken from each lender at a particular moment or reporting date many days or weeks ago. Once the loan information is gathered from each lender, the credit agencies compile our credit report. We can improve our future credit score by understanding this process and identifying the reporting dates with each of our creditors.

The loan information is sent from each creditor to the credit agencies at various times during the month. Most creditors report the loan information to the credit agencies once a month, generally at the end of the month. A few lenders report weekly while others report bi-monthly. Some creditors compile their account information days before reporting to the credit agencies, while others report the account information as it appears on the reporting day. This date is the moment of truth when the individual picture is taken! It is the date when our balance, payment history, along with any additional pertinent account information will show up in our credit report — usually between 15 to 45 days after the individual picture is taken. This is the date of judgment — when the credit score is determined. So, we need to make it look our best!

Many of us hurt our credit scores month after month by failing to recognize the reporting dates for each account. We consistently carry a high balance through the reporting date even though we may pay down the balance immediately after the reporting period. Since our future credit scores are impacted, we must be cognizant of these reporting dates. If our loan balances are lower at that reporting date each month, our individual picture looks better resulting in a higher credit score. We can make principal balance payments to our loans before those reporting dates instead of the billing due dates. This can be a small but very effective practice to consistently raise our scores higher over time.

The Reporting Process

Each creditor reports the loan information including current account balance, amount of last payment, on-time payment, and any loan changes and sends all of it to the credit agencies on the reporting date. Two reporting examples are given.

Example #1

XYZ Credit Card account on January 20, 2006

Account Number	Credit Limit	Balance	Payment History
1234567	1000	800	Current

XYZ Reporting Date to the credit agencies: January 20, 2006

Credit Report Date: March 1, 2006

Account reflects a balance of $800 on the March 1, 2006 credit report with a reporting date of January 2006. The revolving balance ratio is 80% negatively impacting scores for upwards of 30 days until the account information is updated form the February 2006 account update.

Example #2

XYZ Credit Card paid off on January 21, 2006

Account Number	Credit Limit	Balance	Payment History
1234567	1000	0	Current

XYZ Reporting Date to the credit agencies: January 25, 2006

Credit Report Date: March 1, 2006

Account reflects a balance of $0 on the March 1, 2006 credit report with a reporting date of January 2006. The revolving balance ratio is 0% positively impacting credit scores. Since the second example reports its information on January 25 instead of January 20 for XYZ, the account information reflects a $0 balance on the March 1, 2006 report.

If we make payments on or before the reporting date, we can reduce our balances on our loans and we can consistently have higher credit scores. This is an especially effective strategy for those who pay off a credit card account balance monthly.

32. Payment Due Dates

Create a credit file that has a perfect payment record

The one single factor with the greatest impact in raising our credit score is on-time payments. Although on-time payments is not the sole factor in automatically raising our credit score, it is the most important factor above all other reasons. Building a credit file that has a perfect payment history is critical to building our scores.

We first should know when the payment due dates are and when a late payment will be reported to our credit report. Some incorrectly believe that once a loan has incurred a late fee, that lender will automatically report a late payment on their credit. In most cases, this is not true. Each lender has a late fee date and a date when a payment is reflected as late on the credit. They are usually two separate dates. Late fees are usually assessed before late payments are reported on our credit. The dates when late payments are reported to our credit depends on the loan type.

Mortgage, auto, and other installment loans usually report a 30-day late payment when a payment is received 30 to 59 days after the missed payment's due date. A 60-day late payment is two payments behind or when a payment is received 60 to 89 days after the first missed payment's due date. A 90-day late payment is three payments in arrears or a payment is received 90 days to 119 days after the first missed payment's due date. If no payments are made, the lender will continue to report the account 120 days (four months behind) and 150 days (five months behind) late on our credit. Once the payments are six months behind or 180 days past due the first missed payment, the loan is a complete loss to the lender, and a *'9'* is reported to our credit file.

There is a greater variance on reported late payments from creditors who offer revolving lines of credit. Credit card, home equity, or other revolving account lenders usually report one 30-day late when the payment is 30 days past the due date. However, some lenders report a 30-day late anywhere from one day up to 60 days past the missed payment's due date. We should inquire with the lender to know exactly when a missed payment on a revolving loan will be reported late.

Credit agencies retain all the payment information in our files for up to seven years. When we have even one late payment, it can drop our score for years with *"Level of delinquency on accounts"* (2). An 800 level credit score requires a perfect payment history on every loan for at least seven years. With a perfect on-time payment history, we can more easily address any other issues in our credit report.

Payment History

**There are two systems used to report our payment history. We must iden-
tify which reporting system is being used to understand our payment history. The two systems are outlined.**

With both payment history system examples, the same account is used and the credit
report is requested in June 2006. The loan is currently 150 days or five months past
due. The account was current up until five months ago. The account was 30 days late in
February 2006, two months past due in March 2006, three months past due in April
2006, four months past due in May 2006, and is currently five months past due in June
2006. The following symbols represent a current payment and the number of payments
the account was past due with both reporting systems.

System 1

Credit Report Date: *June 1, 2006*

Account	Reporting Date	Opening Date	Payment	Payment History
ABC	6/06	6/04	25	54321CCCCCCC
				CCCCCxCCCCCC
				(6/06 - 5) (5/06 - 4)

Symbols	Meaning
C	*Payments have been current.*
1	*Payment was 30 days late or one payment past due.*
2	*Payment was 60 days late or two payments past due.*
3	*Payment was 90 days late or three payments past due.*
4	*Payment was 120 days late or four payments past due.*
5	*Payment was 150 days late or five payments past due.*
9	*Payment is 180 days late and is charged off as a complete loss for the lender.*
X	*No payment activity.*

System 2

Credit Report Date: *June 1, 2006*

Account	Reporting Date	Opening Date	Payment	Payment History
ABC	6/06	6/04	25	654321111111
				11111x111111
				(6/06 - 6) (5/06 - 5)

Symbols	Meaning
1	*Payments have been current.*
2	*Payment was 30 days late or one payment past due.*
3	*Payment was 60 days late or two payments past due.*
4	*Payment was 90 days late or three payments past due.*
5	*Payment was 120 days late or four payments past due.*
6	*Payment was 150 days late or five payments past due.*
9	*Payment is 180 days late and is charged off as a complete loss for the lender.*
X	*No payment activity.*

33. New Loans

Limit new loans to no more than one a year

Every time we open a new account, we go through a process to open that loan. We apply for the loan, we are approved and sign a promissory note to make timely payments for the loan, and we start making payments. Each step is a process and impacts our score at every level. Recognizing how each step affects our scores can help us better determine the impact of opening new loans on our scores.

Unless we are building our credit, we should space multiple new loans. The application process of the loan requires the lender to pull a copy of our credit report. We then have an inquiry reflected from that lender and *"Too many inquiries"* (8) can impact our scores. When we are approved and sign the papers on the loan, the new loan reflects on our credit record usually within a month. *"Time since recent account opening is too short"* (30) or *"Too many accounts recently opened"* (9) usually at that time appears as a factor impacting our score. These factors can all combine to affect our credit score for several months.

These issues impact our credit score because we are taking on new debt and we have not established a proven payment record with the new loan. Opening multiple loans over a short period of time will continue to increase our credit risk and lower our scores. Understanding this process should help us recognize to spread out new loans. Otherwise, the decline in our scores over the coming year can be substantial.

We can't entirely stop from opening new loans. We may have to finance a new auto, take out a student loan for college, or refinance a mortgage. Once we have an established credit file with at least three open quality accounts, we should space any new mortgage, auto, or educational loans to one every 12 months. Revolving accounts should be spaced even farther; one new account every 24 months. Otherwise, our drive to 800 can be detoured for the next few years until those new accounts have matured.

Those of us who are self-employed, have a new credit file, or are reestablishing credit, must usually open several loans within a short periods of time. If new loans are having a substantial impact on our scores and we have an established number of accounts, we should payoff and close those loans that have recently been opened. By limiting the number of accounts we open annually, we can avoid creating a roller coaster credit score.

34. Mature Loans

We should follow the 75/25 rule

Many of us transfer our debt to newly opened accounts with lower interest rates. A common mistake is constantly closing older, more established accounts to open new loans. This revolving door can constantly disrupt a score's progression higher. There are two reason codes that target the age of our open accounts. *"Length of time revolving accounts have been established"* (12 - referenced on page 52) and *"Length of time accounts have been established"* (14) are the two issues that factor into our scores. These factors emphasize the need to follow the 75/25 rule with our open accounts.

We have two similar loans with one difference. One mortgage is two years old and a second mortgage is ten years old. Which loan adds greater value to our credit scores? That mortgage which has been opened the longest provides the greater value. Length builds depth, and depth builds a credit score. *"Length of time accounts have been established"* (14) is based on the average age of current open accounts determined by the opening date on each open account. This issue highlights two emphasis already reviewed with prior strategies. We should establish multiple golden accounts (page 52) and space new loans (page 76). The longer our accounts have been open, the higher our credit scores.

Installment loans and revolving accounts are quite different. Installment loans have a pre-determined time that the account will be open. For example, mortgage loans can be open up to 30 years (some instances even 40 years), auto loans up to six years, personal loans up to five years, and education loans for up to ten years or more depending on the number of deferred payments. For revolving accounts, these accounts can stay open indefinitely in most cases if we at least periodically use the account. A home equity loan (which is still considered a revolving account) usually has a pre-determined length of time it will be open.

The 75/25 rule gives some guidance for a credit score in the 800s. First, we should have at least 75% of all our open accounts with a minimum of four years in age. Second, we should have at least 25% of our open loans with an age greater than seven years. By following this rule, we can avoid length of time as an impacting issue with our credit scores.

If we are establishing a credit file, length of time usually appears as an issue until the majority of our accounts are open for several years. In many situations, our scores will be limited to the higher 600s or lower 700s until we have aged our current accounts.

35. Credit Utilization

Lower this percentage as much as possible

There are revolving balance ratios, loan balance ratios and the last can be called the utilization ratio. What is a utilization ratio? It tells how the amount of debt we have versus the amount we could have if we had our loan balances at their highest levels. Understanding the utilization ratio helps us better understand our overall level of debt.

The *'utilization ratio'*, or the summation of all loan balances to the total of high credit limits on all open revolving accounts, and the initial loan amounts on installment loans and collection accounts, is a substantial factor affecting our credit scores. *"Amount owed on accounts is too high"* (1) appears when we have multiple account balances that are high. Our utilization of credit is high and poses a risk negatively impacting scores.

To calculate this ratio, we first add all the balances owing on mortgages, auto and personal loans, credit cards, and any other account including collections that are showing on the credit report. The total of balances can also be found in the Credit Summary section of the credit report under *Total Balances*. This is the total credit used.

Second, we should total all the high credit limits on all open revolving, installment and other types of loans. We break this down into two parts - revolving, and installment and other loans. We can identify the revolving loans by the *'Rev'* under loan type. We should tally all the high credit limits reflected on the credit report on each open revolving account. We then add the initial loan amounts on all currently open installment, mortgage, and other accounts. These loans are open and count against the utilization ratio when they have a current balance greater than 0. We then add the total of the high credit limits and the initial loan amounts together. This is the total available credit to us.

The third and final step is to take the total credit used (Step 1) and divide it into the total available credit (Step 2). This is what can be referred to as the *'Utilization ratio'*. It defines how much credit we are using that is available to us. When this ratio is above 80 and especially 90 percent, this issue can truly affect our scores. The lower this ratio, the less impact and higher the credit score. The residual effect emanates throughout our credit score profile. This concern usually arises when we take out multiple consumer installments loans over a short period of time or we have multiple credit cards and other lines of credit with excessive high debt ratios.

The utilization ration, even though not used specifically by the credit scoring system, gives us a better picture on how we are handling our debt load. Are we keeping our balances low and spacing out new loans; or are we raising our debts on our credit cards and taking out multiple new auto, personal, and other loans within a short period of time. This ratio has some parallel effect as the debt ratio and the loan balance ratio. It provides us with a greater understanding of our credit situation. The lower this ratio, the higher the score and vice versus.

Utilization Ratio

There are three examples of calculating the utilization ratio. The ratio is calculated by adding the high credit limits / initial loan balances from all the open revolving, installment, and other accounts in the credit file.

Example 1

Companies	Credit Limit	Balance	Ratio
BCD Mortgage	$100,000	$98,000	98%
EFG Auto Financing	$15,000	$15,000	100%
LMN Auto Lenders	$12,000	$10,500	88%
XYZ Credit Card	$5,000	$4,700	94%
WXY Credit Card	$1,000	$900	90%
Utilization Ratio	**133,000**	**129,100**	**97%**

Example 2

Companies	Credit Limit	Balance	Ratio
BCD Mortgage	$100,000	$89,000	89%
EFG Auto Financing	$15,000	$12,000	80%
LMN Auto Lenders	$12,000	$9,000	75%
XYZ Credit Card	$5,000	$3,000	60%
WXY Credit Card	$1,000	$0	0%
Utilization Ratio	**133,000**	**113,000**	**85%**

Example 3

Companies	Credit Limit	Balance	Ratio
BCD Mortgage	$100,000	$70,000	70%
EFG Auto Financing	$15,000	$5,000	33%
LMN Auto Lenders	$12,000	$4,000	33%
XYZ Credit Card	$5,000	$1,000	20%
WXY Credit Card	$1,000	$200	20%
Utilization Ratio	**133,000**	**80,200**	**60%**

Example 1 has a high utilization ratio at 97%, the second example is at 85%, and the third is at 61%. The first example would negatively impact scores more than examples two or three. The best example to raise credit scores is example 3 because the ratio is much lower than example one or two.

36. Open Accounts

Avoid an excessive number of accounts open

The credit scores system only issue two warnings when we have too many accounts open even without a balance. *"Too many bank or national revolving accounts"* (4 - addressed on page 60) and *"Number of established accounts"* (28) both can figure into our scores when we have an excessive number. If we have too many open accounts, we can raise our level of risk and drop our scores.

We already addressed the concern of having a minimum amount of loan activity and creating some depth in our credit file. The number of accounts open is considered another potential risk to our scores if we have an excessive number. *How many open accounts is too much? "Number of established accounts"* (28) appears when we have too many open accounts. What is the correct level? For an 800 score, we should have no more than ten open accounts. This includes mortgages, auto and education loans, credit cards, overdraft accounts and collections.

The number of loans depends on the types of loans that are open in our credit report. If we have a mortgage or installment, the account must have a outstanding balance to be open. Collection accounts will show up under other accounts and must also have a balance to be open. Revolving accounts on the other hand do not have to have a balance to be open. Since credit card lenders like to keep their accounts open indefinitely., we can have several long forgotten accounts still open.

If this issue is affecting our credit score, we should review each account in our entire credit report to identify all the open accounts. We need to look for revolving accounts that may be open long after we have used them. To identify such accounts, we should first look for a reporting date with a recent month and year usually within 90 days of the credit report date.

When we find such accounts, if these accounts do not have written, *"Account closed"* next to the account, there is a good chance that account is still open. We may erroneously think that the account is closed because we no longer utilize it.

Once we have located all the open accounts in our credit report, we can chose those to close. Those revolving accounts that are open the shortest length of time, are not used, and are from a finance company should be targeted first for closure. If we have too many open accounts, we will resolve this concern as we close them.

37. Loans with Balances

Prevent an excessive number of accounts with balances

The sixth and final measurement of outstanding debt used by the credit scoring system is the number of accounts in our credit report with balances. This figure is different from the number of accounts open in that it usually is less, but has a greater impact on our scores. We need to pay particular attention to limit the number of accounts with balances in our credit report.

We can have a mortgage, an auto loan, and a couple of credit cards. All these accounts count against our scores if we have an excessive number of loans with balances. *"Too many accounts with balances"* (5) is a common warning sign when we have an excessive number of revolving and installment loans with outstanding balances. Such loans include mortgages, credit cards, home equity loans, education loans, auto loans, personal loans, credit cards, personal lines of credit, overdraft accounts, and collections. Every account with a balance showing on our credit report counts.

We may have purchased a home and used two mortgages to lower our monthly payments. We may have purchased a car and have an auto loan. We may have multiple credit card or merchant accounts with balances from recent purchases. We may even have a medical collection or two. One account could have $250,000 balance while another has a $1 balance. They all count and impact our total number of accounts with balances in our credit scores.

What is the correct number of loans with balances we should have for an 800 or higher credit score? We should try to have four or less accounts with balances. As our credit score climbs, the number of accounts with balances could even be reduced to three or two. We may have a mortgage, an auto loan and maybe one credit card for monthly expenses. As we limit the number of active accounts with balances, we will see increases in our score.

If *"Too many account with balances"* (5) is impacting our score, we should look at possibilities to reduce the number of loans outstanding. We could payoff the smaller balance accounts, or consolidate loans. We may consolidate our credit card accounts as long we don't exceed a 50% debt ratios or have a credit card balance greater than $2,500. If we have the equity, we may even take out a home equity line of credit to consolidate our balances. We have options. We simply need to find the best workable solution to reduce this risk factor in our credit score.

38. Auto Purchases

Negotiate sales price, not monthly payments or incentives

"We finance everyone!" or *"Bad credit, no credit, no problem!"* are marketing slogans from auto salesmen. Many critical mistakes happen when we allow auto salesmen to arrange our auto loans. Auto dealerships often make more money on auto financing than they profit from selling us the car. When auto salesmen determine our lender and loan, they can negatively impact our scores.

Salesmen obviously don't look for the lowest interest rate or monthly payment. They look for the lender that will pay them, the salesman, the most money for our loan. If a lender for example offers us a 5% interest rate on a $15,000 five year auto loan, we would pay $283.07 a month. The total of payments would be $16,984.20. Instead, the salesmen offers us a 9% interest rate for $311.38 a month. The total of payments would be $18,682.80. The difference between the two loans over the five year term is $1,698.60.

A common agreement has the auto lender paying auto salesmen $75 for an extra $100 charged to the borrower. With this example, the lender would pay the salesman $1,273.95 (75% of extra interest) in addition to any set up and processing fees (say $500), for a total of $1,773.95. In the end, the auto dealership can make a lot more money if we allow them to set up our loan.

Additionally, the business relationship between auto dealers and lenders is very strong. Buyers are often approved for loans considerably more than the vehicle's worth. These lenders almost never deny a loan from the dealer because of this close business relationship. They add the extra risk by offering a higher sales price or interest rate resulting in higher loan payments. When we try to sell the car or refinance the loan, the balance is considerable higher than the car's value and we are stuck.

Finally, auto lenders in many cases are true finance companies which can negatively impact our credit scores *(See Strategy 17)*. Finance companies use auto dealerships as one of their sources for new business. Even taking out a loan with one of them and refinancing the auto loan two months later can be problematic. We could have already damaged our credit making it less possible to refinance the loan.

The only loan offered by the auto dealership that can be attractive is a manufacturer's loan from *Honda*, *Ford*, *GMAC, etc...*. Otherwise, we should have our own lender before walking onto the car lot.

Tips *to Purchasing an Auto*

1. **Determine an auto's value by researching a car's value.**
    -- We can go to a website such as www.autotrader.com or other websites and research specific trade-in and retail values on cars. We can prevent taking out a loan substantially more than the car's worth.

2. **Be pre-approved from our lender for an auto loan before starting the search.**
    -- Don't let the auto dealer arrange our auto financing. Once approved, we can proceed to look for a vehicle.

3. **Never let the auto salesmen know that we are already pre-approved.**
    -- Auto salesmen are very savvy. Turn the tables by letting them know we plan on financing the auto. However, never let them know we have our loan already pre-approved until after the final sales price is determined and the contract is signed to purchase the vehicle.

4. **Negotiate our final sales price.**
    -- Sometimes, it is better to walk away for a day or two before purchasing the auto to gain more concessions from the auto salesmen.

5. **Once the final price is determined and the contract is signed, tell the salesmen that your loan is already approved with a lender.**
    -- The salesman may give us additional discounts on the vehicle if he thinks he is arranging the financing. Once the contract is signed and we give notice to the auto salesman that the loan has already arranged, the auto salesman will have a difficult time backing out on the negotiated sales price.

These tips simply mean that the buyers can negotiate a better price for the vehicle, and determine their own lender with a quality interest rate on the loan. The salesman cannot control the loan and make more money by raising the interest rate from the dealer's own lender.

There is one caveat from an auto dealership. The only attractive loans usually offered by the auto dealership are those directly financed by the manufacturer. They sometimes offer interest rates that are considerably lower than current markets rates. However, we should realize that the manufacturer in most cases, simply raises the sales price to offset the lower interest rate.

39. Home Purchases

Avoid conflicts of interest with the seller or builder

One of the most valued credit references we can have for our score is an active mortgage. As a mortgage balance is paid down over time, this quality credit reference can really drive our score higher. Nevertheless, prospective homeowners must protect themselves from scrupulous home sale's agents and builders who oversell their homes. The possible outcomes could cost the us literally thousands of dollars over time and a quality credit score.

The parties usually include an over-zealous seller, home sales agent, or builder, and a their in-house mortgage company. The parties offer so-called *free* closing costs, home upgrades, or other incentives if we simply use their mortgage company. This package can be extremely attractive when offered to new home buyers.

However, we should remember the phrase, *"Nothing in life is free."* The sellers simply raise the cost for upgrades, or increase the home's sales price. Similar to auto salesmen, the seller's mortgage lender can charge more fees for closing or even raise the interest rate to recover those so-called free items. We may soon discover that those free items are not so free after all. When the seller has us over a barrel after the contract is signed, we learn that the items offered in the showroom are four times more expensive than at the local hardware store, closing costs are more, and interest rates are higher.

The results can potentially be devastating with higher than anticipated monthly payments. We might have to quickly sell or refinance the mortgage and discover the home is vastly overpriced. Our chances of falling behind on payments increase. The end result could be late payments or even foreclosure.

We should be extremely cautious when there is only one mortgage company, one appraiser, or one title company and in an established business relationship. We may never know that there is a problem until we sell the home or refinance the loan.

Buying a home is important. Avoiding conflicts of interest with sellers and their affiliated companies is critical to prevent being caught in a trap that could add unnecessary risks to our financial stability and credit score. Home buyers should never let the seller control their financing. They are representing the seller, not our best interests!

Tips *to Purchasing an Home*

1. **Find a quality lender and be pre-approved before searching.**

   --Most mortgage lenders do not offer all the major loan programs especially for first-time homebuyers. Find a quality lender that offers all the major loan programs. Such programs include Federal Housing Administration (FHA), Veteran's Administration (VA), and other local government sponsored loan programs. Ask a lender if they offer such programs before applying. Review all of them to determine the best possible loan for us.

2. **Use a qualified real estate agent.**

   -- Many agents are fairly new or sell real estate as their part time job. Ask for recommendations from friends or family. Be careful when the agent recommends a title or escrow company, or mortgage lender. Ask the agent if they have a business relationship including financial, marketing, or other in which the lenders pays their marketing or for mortgage loans referred to them. Even though this practice is usually prohibited by federal law, there is limited to no enforcement and the practice is quite common. The agent then is less interested in the client and more interested in making additional money by using a specific company because they can receive a kick-back.

3. **When building a new home, sign a generic contract with the general contractor.**

   -- Most builder contracts are very protective of the builder. When negotiating and signing a final contract, we should use a generic contract. Most states have a generic contract that can be used for purchasing a home. Use this contract to avoid all the specific language in contracts that can cause problems later on. Common clauses in builder contracts include the use of specific sub-contractors, mortgage lenders and title companies. Even though a home buyer may be able to buy an item cheaper, the builder's contract may prohibit a buyer from doing so. Negotiate the sales price and the add-ons to the house before signing the contract. Even if we have to walk away and come back another day, you may be better off. This can save a lot of money — even tens of thousands of dollars.

4. **Select your own appraiser and inspector.**

   -- Never let the seller, seller's agent, or seller's lender determine the appraiser. We should have one independent of the seller to insure the sales price is not over-inflated. This simple but effective action can prevent us from taking out a loan that is much than the home's value and condition. Make sure you are getting fair value for our home and that if we had to re-sell the home, we would not have to bring in tens of thousands of dollars to pay off the mortgage.

40. Exotic Mortgages

◆━━━━━━━━━━━━━━━━━━━━━━━━━━━━━━━━━━━━━━━◆

Know the terms and changes in payments and balances

Many real estate agents and mortgage lenders try to convince us to purchase a home with low, affordable, monthly payments. To offer these low monthly payments, lenders advertise payments which include future rate adjustments resulting in higher monthly payments. We can be caught in one of these exotic mortgages and quickly fall behind on such imposing payments, severely impacted our score.

To identify an exotic mortgage, a loan has terms that inevitably increase in payment at some future point or fail to pay down the loan balance. These mortgages include adjustable rate mortgages, interest-only payments, option ARMs (adjustable rate mortgages), and buy downs. (See *Tips to purchasing a home)* The question is, *"When and how much?"*. We should know when and how high the monthly payment adjustments could possibly be.

Payments can increase 10, 20, or even 50%. When payments increase, they can put a financial strain on our budget. We can fall behind on payments raising our credit risk from *"Level of delinquency on accounts"* (2), or even *"Serious delinquency"* (39). In addition, these loans often fail to reduce our principal balances or may even increase them elevating our credit risk from *"Proportion of balances to loan limits is too high"* (33 - EQX / XPN & 3 - TU).

Most real estate professionals and mortgage lenders do not really understand the terms of these mortgages. They are more interested in the sale, not the financing. Since these professionals often don't know them, the general public is less likely to understand them until it is too late.

An adjustable rate mortgage has payment changes that can go higher. Interest-only loans only require us to pay the interest that accrues and there is usually no balance reduction. A buy down has teaser payments for the first few years of the loan. Last of all, the Option ARM has payment options that don't even pay the interest that has accrued. We can actually owe more within a year or two than we initially borrowed.

We should never rely upon a home sales agent for mortgage payment information. Instead, we should review the payment programs with a qualified independent mortgage lender to avoid future payment shock. A complete understanding now can help alleviate any misunderstanding and possible future late payments.

Exotic Mortgages

1. Buy Down Mortgage

-- A buy down is a lower monthly payment for the first 12, 24, or 36 months of a loan. The actual note rate and interest rate on the loan never changes (unless a variable rate loan). Rather, the amount of interest paid by the homeowner changes usually every 12 months. A buy down simply provides the homeowner with a lower payment for a certain period of time.

For example, a person with a fixed interest rate of 7.00% with a 2-1 buy down on a $150,000 loan would have a monthly principal and interest payment of $997.95. With a 2-1 buy down, the first year's payment would be calculated at 5.00% or $805.23 a month, the second year 6.00% or $899.33 a month, and the third year and be yond, 7.00% or $997.95 a month.

However, a buy down must have funds supplemented from some source to work. Since the interest rate is always 7.00% and the home owner is only paying 5.00% the first year, and 6.00% the second year, funds must be generated to make up the difference in interest owed. The interest owed would be 2.00% the first year or $192.72 a month, and 1.00% the second year or $98.62 a month. An escrow account of $3,496.44 (12 months times 192.72 plus 12 months times 98.62) is set up at closing from contributions from either the buyer and / or seller to make the extra interest payment on the loan.

2. Adjustable Rate Mortgage

-- An adjustable rate mortgage is a loan that at some point will have future interest rate and payment adjustments. The payment adjustments can be within a month, or as long as ten years from the beginning of the loan. The more common adjustable rate mortgages usually have rate adjustments between six months up to five years.

The future interest rate adjustments are determined by the index, margin, and adjustment caps established at the beginning of the loan. An adjustable rate mortgage has a starting fixed rate of 5.00% for the first three years, a margin of 2.75%, a cap of 5.00%, and an index tied to the one year US Treasury bond. If the US Treasury bond is 4.50% in year three, the borrower rate will adjust to 6.75%. The rate on the note will then make adjustments every pre-determined period of time (usually six to 12 months).

Terms
Index - The index determines the future interest rate adjustments.
Margin - The margin is the add to the index to determine the future interest rate.
Cap - A cap is the most an interest rate can increase or decrease during a certain period of time even if the interest rate determined from the index plus margin is higher or lower than the cap. .

Exotic Mortgages

3. Interest-Only Mortgage

-- An interest-only mortgage can have either a fixed or variable interest rate. The difference with this loan is the payment for a certain period of time is only interest, and not principal and interest. This can make a payment lower, but also cause future payments to increase.

An interest-only loan has an initial balance of $200,000 with an interest rate of 5.50% for the first five years. The minimum payment for those first five years would be $916.67 instead of $1,135.58 if the loan was principal and interest at the same rate. In most cases, the interest-only rates are usually lower than fixed rate mortgages.

At the end of the five years, the payment could jump to $1,228.18 if no principal was paid down during those five years. The reason that the payment would jump is because the payment resets after the five year period and starts requiring a principal and interest payment for the remaining 25 years on the principal owing.

In many situations, the interest-only loan is also a variable rate mortgage. The payment goes up even more if short-term rates are higher. They are highly speculative mortgages and anyone looking at an interest-only loan should understand the terms before signing the loan documents.

4. Option ARM (Adjustable Rate Mortgage)

-- This mortgage has an adjustable interest rate and provides the borrower with an option of what payment to make. Four options are usually available to chose from. There are regular consistent payments as calculated over the term of the loan, a principal and interest payment on the current interest rate, a minimum monthly payment, and an interest-only payment.

The minimum monthly payment can result in a negative amortized loan in which the loan balance increases because the monthly payment does not cover the interest accrued during that month. The interest-only is similar to the interest-only mortgage in that we can c h o s e to make just the interest payment.

We can make a choice each month which payment to make. The interest accrued may change since the loans are adjustable rate mortgages. In addition, the minimum monthly payment has some limitations when the loan balance increases to 110% of the original loan.

41. Free Credit Reports

Periodically request a report to review your credit files

Misunderstanding and misinformation about the free credit reports is a common problem among the general public. To assist us with our credit files, Congress recently passed the Fair Credit Reporting Act (known as the FACT Act) in 2003 which allows everyone the right to one free annual credit report from each credit bureaus. We should utilize this opportunity to review the information from each credit report.

The FACT Act requires the major credit bureaus to send each of us a free copy of our credit report upon request. These free annual reports help us to become better educated and to review for misinformation on our report and to recognize any signs of identity theft. Each credit report is usually different. Not every creditor reports to all three credit bureaus. Every few months, we should periodically review our credit report from each credit agency. We can rotate between the three credit bureaus throughout the year. By requesting our free credit report every four months, we can better track our credit files for any unauthorized access or even for identity theft.

These free reports however do not provide the credit score. The credit bureaus charge money for scores. It is a huge income generating source for the credit bureaus. The major credit bureaus even make it difficult to request a free credit report without ordering our credit score. If we cannot find the exact location on the website to order our free credit report, we should simply write the credit bureaus to request our free report and avoid the cost.

One other report we should request once a year is from *Choicepoint*. *Choicepoint* reports are used by insurance companies, employers, and landlords. These reports help determine our insurance premiums, assist with any landlord decisions, and provide our employment history. We should request their report (which is free) to review our background information for accuracy.

Other companies now and in the future are and will be compiling information on us. We can request a free personal report since many of these companies must abide by the Fair Credit Reporting Act. It will help us keep tabs on the information that is being generated on us.

Credit Bureaus

We can request a free annual credit report from each of the three major credit bureaus. However, they will not disclose the credit score unless we pay for it.

Equifax

Address	PO Box 740241
	Atlanta, Georgia 740241
Telephone Number	800-685-1111
Website	www.annualcreditreport.com
	www.equifax.com/fcra

Experian

Address	PO Box 2002
	Allen, Texas 75013-0036
Telephone Number	888-397-3742
Website	www.annualcreditreport.com
	www.experian.com

Trans Union

Address	PO Box 1000
	Chester, Pennsylvania 19022
Telephone Number	800-888-4213
Website	www.annualcreditreport.com
	www.transunion.com

Choicepoint

Telephone Numbers:	
Insurance	866-312-8076
Employment	866-312-8075
Tenant	877-448-5732
Website	www.choicetrust.com

We must usually go to the website, www.annualcreditreport.com to receive a free copy of our credit report. However, the website is full of offers to sign up for credit monitoring services. If we cannot locate where to request the free credit report online, we can send a letter with name, address, social security number, and picture identification requesting our free credit report. Choicepoint is also considered a data collection agency. They do not issue credit reports, but rather provide background reports to insurance companies, employers, and landlords. We can also ask for our free personal reports from them.

10

Common Errors

John and Suzie were building a new home. They both had credit scores in the mid-700s and John had a solid income, limited debt and an overall quality profile. They had no problem being approved for their construction loan. After six months of construction, the house was completed and they updated their loan application to complete their long-term mortgage. To our complete surprise, John's credit score had suddenly dropped during construction and was now in the low 500's.

A Chapter 7 bankruptcy came out of nowhere and was now showing on John's credit report. He had never filed bankruptcy, but not according to his credit report. After several days, he tracked down the culprit. A clerk at the bankruptcy court had transposed two digits in a social security number and the bankruptcy now showed up on his credit report. A bad mistake had happened at a bad time.

He had to document the problem and after a few weeks of delay, he was able to still be approved for their mortgage. Nevertheless, John continued to have problems trying to correct the information on his credit report. It took him several months before the bankruptcy was finally removed. He still had fears, and reason so, that the bankruptcy would reappear to cause future problems with his scores.

A recent report by the *National Association of State PIRGs* identifies the common problem of inaccuracies in credit reports. This report found that 79% of all credit reports contained some type of error. Some errors were minor, while others were a huge factor in determining the credit scores. Even further, 25% of all credit reports were found to have such serious errors contained in them, that they greatly affected a person's loan qualification. Since credit bureaus manage hundreds of millions of credit files and billions of pieces of information every month, we should always be proactive to limit the errors in our credit reports.

Anyone who regularly reviews his credit can attest that there are usually multiple inaccuracies in most credit files. Inaccurate information in credit files occurs in different forms. There can be late payments that were never late, accounts that have been requested to be closed that are still open, duplicate loans, missing information, incorrect balances, mis-application of credit scoring information, along with other inaccuracies. Where there is inaccurate information, the problems can persist and credit scores are dramatically impacted.

Borrowing costs and the chances of having a loan denied increases from inaccurate reports and scores. The problem of credit misinformation is a constant problem that takes an active and informed person to control it. Credit scores can be influenced by numerous pieces of misinformation in each account. Any slight misstep can result in a lower score.

There are no universal road signs that will point us to the right direction. Everyone's situation is different. Correcting a credit report with our corresponding score can be extremely challenging and frustrating. If we recognize common caution signs, we can better detect common errors and correct them.

This chapter identifies the more common mistakes we may find in credit files. By identifying these common problems, we can be better informed and the corrections when needed to protect credit scores.

42. Creditors

―――――――――――――――――――――――――――――――――――――――

Identify all the creditors in our report

When we receive a copy of our credit report, one of the first tasks we should do is to review the list of creditors in the account history section. A thorough review helps us recognize any inaccurate information or unauthorized access to our credit file.

Creditors are usually listed on the left side of the report. Each account should be examined for inaccurate lenders, misuse, or identity theft. The initial company that processed our loan may not be the lender listed on our credit report. Companies often sell our loans or report to the credit bureaus under unfamiliar names. The chief concern is to identify all the active accounts or loans with balances, or any accounts with late payments. Active revolving accounts have a *'Last Active Date'* or a *'Reporting Date'* that is usually within the last 60 to 90 days of the credit report date while installment loans have a balance owing.

Common errors occur when people have similar social security numbers and names, have a co-signed account, or show an ex-spouse's loans. If an erroneous account is discovered on our credit report, we should contact that creditor to investigate the error. A written dispute should also be sent to the credit bureaus requesting that they correct our credit files. We may have to send multiple disputes before the inaccuracy is ultimately corrected in our credit report.

A credit report should be requested a couple of months after the information has been disputed to make sure the error is corrected and does not reappear. If the account remains, the problem could be originating from the lender. A request to the lender to remove the account may be necessary before the information will be corrected. By staying proactive, we can protect our credit reports from such common errors.

Common Account Names

Creditor	Name	Creditor	Name
CBUSASEARS	Sears	HSBC / RS	Radio Shack
WF Fin	Wells Fargo Finance	GEMB / Mervyns	Mervyns
GEMB / JCP	JCPenney	WFNNB / Lerner	Lerner
GECAP / Sams	Sams Club	WFNNB / Victoria	Victoria Secret
Washmtl / Prov	Providian	GE	GE Credit Card
Benfcl	Beneficial	UNVL / Citi	Citifinancial
Amex	American Express	WFNNB / Lane Bry	Lane Bryant
WFB CD Svc	Wells Fargo Credit Card	FCNB / Spiegel	Spiegel
RNB Target	Target	HHld Bank	Household Bank
Associates / Citi	Citifinancial	MCCBG / Gap	The Gap

43. Duplicate Accounts

Review outstanding loans for duplication

A constant problem with lenders and credit bureaus is duplicate loans. We may have one loan, but the credit file reports multiple, active loans because of a communication error. Since too many accounts with balances is a factor with scores, we should always look for duplicate loans.

There can be multiple sources to this common problem. More common occurrences happen because of an incorrect account number, the sale of a loan from one lender to another, a refinanced loan, or there is an inability to properly communicate between the lender and the credit bureau. The opening dates, credit limits, balances and other account information can report the same information on both loans.

When a duplicate account is discovered, we must first identify all the credit bureaus listed in the credit report. If a credit report is from just one credit bureau and there are two loans reporting the same account, this is a sign of a duplicate loan. If two or more credit bureaus are included in a single credit report, duplicate loans occur when the identical account is being reported twice by the same credit bureau.

Each loan on the credit report reveals which credit bureau is providing that particular loan information. As given in the example, the same credit bureau, *Experian,* is reporting duplicate information when the bureau shows it acronym *XPN* on both loans (*EQX - Equifax, XPN - Experian, TU - Trans Union*). If two or more loans appear in the same report, but appear under separate credit bureaus, this is not a duplicate loan. Rather the credit report failed (and not the credit bureaus) to properly merge the account from all three credit bureaus into one loan.

If a duplicate loan is discovered, we should submit a letter identifying the problem to both the creditor and the lender. A credit report should be pulled a few months after the correction to verify that the duplicate account has been permanently removed from our credit report.

Companies	Acct No	Balance	Credit Bureau
Before			
ABC Credit Card	3456703	$420	XPN
ABC Credit Card	34567	$420	XPN
After			
ABC Credit Card	3456703	$420	XPN

ABC has the same credit card account reporting twice from Experian until corrected.

44. Open Accounts

Check reporting and last active dates for open loans

Another concern for many of us is those paid off accounts that we may have used many months or years ago which remain open. Creditors often leave these accounts open hoping that we will return and even after we have asked them to close the account. We should review the *Last Active Dates* and the *Reporting Dates* on our credit report to identify any open accounts to reduce their impact on our scores.

One of the main road signs *"Number of established accounts"* (28) is a result from having an excessive number of accounts open. Even though we may not have a balance or even use the accounts, these still active accounts can affect our credit scores for years. Whenever we receive a copy of our credit report, we should review the number of accounts we have open. It is not an easy process since there is nothing in the credit report that says, *"Open Account"*. Rather, open revolving accounts must be identified by a recent *Reporting Date* that has does not state, *"Account Closed"*. Installment loans are closed when they are paid off.

To identify any open accounts, we should look for the *Reporting Date* to be within three months of the credit report date. If the credit bureau date is 6/01/06, open loans reflect a reporting date that is within a couple of months from the credit report date (3/06 to 6/06). If an account reports a recent month and year, chances are that loan is still open. We may have to contact the lender to verify an account is open.

When we want to close an account, we should send a letter to the creditor requesting the account be closed. Otherwise, the lender could leave the account open. Once a revolving account is closed, the account should read *"Account closed"*. Recognizing recent reporting dates without an *"Account closed"* will help us locate any of those unnoticed active accounts. When we have an excessive number of accounts open, looking for unused forgotten accounts should be our first priority.

Credit Report Date: 1/01/2007

Companies	Reporting Date	Balance
Before		
HIJ Credit Card	12/05	$0
After		
HIJ Credit Card	1/07	$0
Account Closed		

HIJ account is an old account still open. The account is closed and reflects on report.

45. High Credit Limits

Failure by companies to report limits can affect scores

One of the most important items to review in our credit report is the *high credit limit* on each outstanding revolving loan. A common practice from credit card companies is to withhold the *high credit limit* on a our credit report. Since a *high credit limit* helps to determine the debt ratio, a failure by lenders to report this critical information can be detrimental to our credit scores.

When a revolving loan's *high credit limit* is not reported correctly to the credit bureau, our credit risk increases and scores decline. *"Proportion of balances to high credit limits too high on revolving accounts"* (10) may appear as a major factor impacting our credit scores. Some credit card companies have been accused of intentionally omitting this information from their account information sent to the credit bureaus. Since this omission is not illegal, lenders who offer revolving lines of credit can make us appear less attractive to fellow competitors. Our credit scores decline and we will have a lesser chance of receiving a better qualifying offer. Lenders have a better chance of retaining our loan since competitors will probably make less attractive offers to us.

Companies know how to manipulate credit scores and they often do it without our knowledge. They may claim that the problem is an error or that their company does not report the *high credit limit* because of some company policy. However, the problem occurs all too often to be unintentional. Who loses? You and I. Who wins? The lender with our loan.

All the revolving accounts should be reviewed for accurate credit limits each time we receive our credit report. When a revolving loan's *high credit limit* is missing or is erroneous, we should contact the lender and demand the *high credit limit* be correctly reported to the credit bureaus. After multiple requests to report the correct credit limit have failed, we may have to file a complaint with the Federal Trade Commission or contact an attorney to correct the problem.

Companies	Credit Limit	Balance	Ratio
Before			
ABC Credit Card	— —	$1,000	$1,000
			over the limit
After			
ABC Credit Card	$2,000	$1,000	*50%*

ABC has no credit limit and shows a debt ratio. Credit limit is subsequently corrected.

46. Incorrect Balances

◆━━━━━━━━━━━━━━━━━━━━━━━━━━━━━━━◆

Review loans for incorrect account balances

We have illustrated the concern when we have too many accounts with balances. Another common error often found in credit reports is incorrect account balances. These errors can include past loans reflecting old balances or active loans that report an erroneous loan amount. A quick review of the balances with the corresponding reporting dates can help us identify loan balances that are inaccurate.

Having excessive loans with balances even though the loan may be old can create additional credit risk. As a result, *"Too many accounts with balances"* (5) can negatively impact our credit scores. Reviewing all the account balances with recent *Reporting Dates* helps us identify any old loan balances in our credit report.

The origin of this problem can be several sources. One problem occurs when an older loan shows an outstanding balance. If an account has a balance and the *Reporting Date* is six months or older, that loan is usually reporting an inaccurate balance. This commonly occurs when a loan is sold or is refinanced, a loan is not updated monthly, or a balance is not cleared following a bankruptcy, settlement or is paid off. When accounts are paid off, lenders tend to leave the last balance owing for years as reported on the last reporting date. Collection companies are notorious for failing to update a paid account.

Another common problem is when a current loan is indicating an incorrect loan balance. If an outstanding loan balance does not reflect an amount within the last 30 to 90 days, the lender may be reporting incorrect information. Incorrect balances may be reported for several reasons. We may have multiple loans with a lender without proper oversight. Lenders may also include the interest due for the entire loan instead of the current balance. This can reflect a much higher loan balance. Whatever the situation, we should always review our balances.

Credit Report Date: 1/01/2007		
Companies	**Reporting Date**	**Balance**
Before		
ADG Credit Card	2/03	$420
After		
ADG Credit Card	1/07	$0
ADG has an old balance reporting as reflect by the reporting date.		

47. Past Due Balances

Review past due column for errors

The *Past due* column in the account section of the credit report identifies any payment or balance amount that is delinquent. Any amount in this column has a substantial negative impact on our scores. However, it is often found with many errors. This column reflects the amount past due with any current or past account. We should always examine this column when reviewing our credit report.

A figure in the *past due* column appears when we are currently delinquent with a payment on an active loan, or we have a collection that is still owing. The *past due* column contains the total amount past due from any payments or series of payments. The payment usually must be 30 or more days late as reflected in the payment history before the creditor reports a past due amount. When we have an amount showing as past due, *"Amount past due on accounts"* (21) is usually the warning sign that appears.

Common errors with the past due column may reflect old account information from loans or collections that were past due and have been settled or paid off for months and even years. It is a serious problem with lenders and collection agencies.

When accounts have been brought current, a collection has been paid, or a bankruptcy has been discharged, we should request a copy of our credit report within 90 days. If old amounts continue to show up in the past due column, we may have to contact the creditor or send a copy of the paid receipt to the credit bureaus. If there has been a bankruptcy, a dispute should be submitted to the credit bureaus requesting that the amounts in the *past due* column should reflect 0.

Removing any inaccurate amounts in this column helps a credit score recover. Unless corrected, this past due amount can hinder credit scores for years to come.

Companies	Balance	Past Due	Payment
Before			
DFG Collection	$700	$70	$0
After			
DFG Collection	$0	$0	$0
This collection is paid and the balance and the past due amounts are updated.			

48. Payment History

Examine report for inaccurate payment histories

Keeping a perfect payment history with our outstanding loans is always a challenge. Nevertheless, inaccurate late payments seem to be a consistent problem even for those individuals who have a spotless credit history. The effect on credit scores from late payments can be extremely damaging. Incorrect payment histories can affect our ability to qualify for any future loan.

Payment histories for most loans are reported to the credit bureau on a monthly basis. The credit file usually displays the payment history for each loan month by month for the last 24 months. Late payments beyond those 24 months may be reflected with the month and year, and how many payments the account was behind.

Credit bureaus report payment histories two separate ways. One method has current payments reporting with 1's and late payments reflected as '2' (30 day late), '3' (60 day late), and so on. The second method reflects current payments with a 'C' (Current) and late payments as '1' (30 day late), '2' (60 day late), and so forth.

When we have had late payments, we should request a payment history from the lender to review their information for accuracy. If a late payment is incorrect, we should copy the canceled checks or transaction record along with the payment history. A copy should be sent both to the lender and the credit bureaus so that the correct information can be reflected in the credit file.

No one should automatically take the word of the lender and the credit bureau with payment histories. Payment histories are sometimes inaccurate. Since late payments can do a lot of damage to credit scores, it is worth the time for us to check their accuracy.

Credit Report Date: 1/01/07			
	Companies	**Reporting Date**	**Payment History**
Method 1	JDF Credit Card	01/07	121111111111
			111111111111
			11/06—30 days
Method 2	JDF Credit Card	01/07	C1CCCCCCCCCC
			CCCCCCCCCCCC
			11/06—30 days
Both accounts show a 30-day late payment for November 2006.			

49. Reporting Errors

Identify source to avoid correcting multiple times

Whenever we discover inaccurate information in our credit report, we should dispute the error with the corresponding credit bureau to correct the error. We can dispute an error and have the issue removed from our credit report, but subsequently find the error reappear on our report after a couple of months. With such cases, we may have to identify the source of the error, or the inaccuracy could reappear.

An inaccuracy is usually caused by an inability of a creditor or other party to properly communicate to the credit bureau. There are generally two common causes of misinformation; lenders or other internal information is incorrect, or a breakdown in communication between the reporting entity and the credit bureau.

If a lender's information is incorrect, the credit report's error is simply illustrating what the lender is reporting. When we try to dispute the information with the credit bureau, the request may come back unchanged. Since the credit bureau verified what the lender is reporting, the dispute with its subsequent investigation simply confirmed the lender's misinformation.

If the inaccuracy is corrected, the credit report may reflect the accurate information until the lender updates the account and reports the error again. This scenario would change the corrected information back to an error. If the error is with the lender, we must have the creditor correct the inaccuracy in their reporting systems.

The more frequent problem occurs when the reporting entity and credit bureaus have failed to properly communicate. We should be able to request the information corrected without much problem. The chances of having the problem reappear are less frequent.

Finding the source of the incorrect information may be half the battle in trying to correct account or public record information. Our frustration can build when an error must be corrected over and over again. Finding the source of the inaccuracy may be just as important as correcting the error itself. When we find errors in our credit report, we should contact those lenders to verify that they are not reporting incorrect account information. We can identify the source of the error and be able to permanently correct a problem much quicker.

50. Derogatory Accounts

Recognize dates when an account drops from the report

Whenever any one of our accounts has had a late payment reported in its payment history, the account status changes from *'Satisfied account'* to a *'Delinquent account'*. That status remains with that account until seven years after the last late payment. However, a common mistake with the credit reporting system is changing a *'Derogatory account'* back to a *'Satisfied account'*.

A derogatory account gives the basis for the credit scoring system to determine a couple of very important factors. *"Number of accounts with delinquency"* (18) *and "Too few accounts currently paid as agreed"* (19 -EQX / XPN & 27 - TU) are the two factors that are based on the number of accounts that have had at least one blemish on their payment record. When there is a clean payment record for seven years, the derogatory mark is supposed to fall from the credit history and the account should be removed from the derogatory account section of the credit report.

In many cases, it is not removed and the status with the account remains even though it has a seven year clean payment record. This problem occurs from two main issues. First, the last late payment remains on the account past the seven years or second, the account status is never changed with the credit bureaus. This inaccuracy can continue to impact scores beyond the allotted time frame.

If we do have a late payment, we need to recognize the month and year when the late payment will fall from the account. It will be seven years from the last late payment. If the payment history has been perfect, we should pull our credit report after the last reporting late payment to verify that the late payment has dropped from the account. The account status should then show as a satisfactory account.

There is a lot of old information that remains on our credit report for years after it is supposed to drop off. With most accounts, it does not impact our credit scores. In some circumstances, such as those described, it can impact our scores. We need to make sure that our report is accurate and that older bad credit history is removed from our credit file in the expected time frame.

51. Disputing Errors

Knowing how to dispute can save us time and money

The profession of disputing information with credit bureaus is a high revenue industry. Companies may charge us substantial amounts of money to correct our credit information. We can save money and achieve practically the same results by understanding how to correct our credit report by properly disputing misinformation in our credit file.

When submitting a dispute letter, we should identify ourselves to the credit bureau with our legal name, valid social security number, current address, and a daytime phone number. The communication should not be long, but rather a short and specific letter identifying ourselves, the creditor, the account number, the error, and the correction requested. We should send our dispute along with a government issued picture identification.

Even though online or phone disputes are available, we are better served if we correspond via a certified letter to verify receipt. Any additional documentation that identifies the error and corroborates the correction should be sent along with the dispute letter. Paid off or satisfaction letters, bankruptcy papers, or other written documentation supplies the credit bureaus with written proof of the error. We should also send a copy of a government issued identification such as a driver's license. By following these simple steps, we can correct most errors in our credit report.

There is a word of caution. If we are trying to remove a bad credit rating from our credit file, there is a chance that this request will actually lead to a lower credit score. If a creditor replies and confirms to the credit bureau that the bad mark is accurate, the credit bureau can update that derogatory account. The *last reporting date* or the *last active date* is then updated to reflect a more recent month with a poor credit rating. This action in many cases will drop a credit score.

If a request to remove a bad credit rating is rejected, we can also irritate the lender. The creditor may give a poorer credit rating than what is already reflected. Unless an attorney is involved, we should only dispute those errors in the credit file. Even with an assistance of an attorney, there is no guarantee that the information will be changed.

Once the investigation is completed, the credit bureaus will send a copy of an updated credit report to us that identifies those changes made in our credit report.

If an error has been corrected, we should request our credit report two or three months later. A mistake can sometimes return even after the error has been corrected. If the error is corrected and then returns after a month or two, the problem could be systematic with either the lender or the credit bureau. If the updated information is still inaccurate or the corrected error has returned to our report, we should send a second dispute letter identifying the inaccuracy. We may have to include a copy of the first findings with the letter of correction.

If a second request does not correct the information, we may need to contact an attorney to send a letter. Credit bureaus and lenders usually pay more attention to an attorney letter. The cost of having a lower score may be substantially more than the cost of an attorney's letter.

By understanding how to dispute and what to expect, we can save a lot of money and time, and be very effective in removing errors from our credit report.

Sample Dispute Letter

Name: John Doe
Social Security Number: 111-22-3344
Address: 1122 Unknown
        Never town, USA 99999

Dear Equifax, Experian, and Trans Union:

Please update the following information in my credit file:

Public Records

Account Name	Case Number	Account Change
ABC Company	3446273	Paid in Full / Satisfied
IRS	20050992811	Paid in Full / Satisfied

Payment History

Creditor	Account Number	Account Change
DEF Company	274873	Paid in Full / $0 Balance
HIJ	4788923	Not my Account
KLM Bank	3529193443	Payment Never Late
NOP	657232	Bankruptcy / $0 Balance
RST	1122331	Paid in Full Before Sent to Collection
UVW	995733	Account Closed / $0 Balance

If you have any questions, please contact me by mail or by phone at
(111) 222-3344.

Thanks,

John Doe (Signature)

Dispute Letter
Common reasons for dispute / under account status

Paid in Full / Satisfied:
> The loan, judgment, collection or tax lien has been paid in full.

Paid in Full / $0 Balance:
> The account has been paid and full and should reflect a $0 balance.

Not my Account:
> The loan, judgment, tax lien, collection, or bankruptcy is not the borrower's information and should be removed.

Payment Never Late / Payment History Inaccurate:
> The account payments on the loan are reporting an inaccurate payment history and should be shown as current (or otherwise)

Account Closed / $0 Balance:
> The account is reporting open with a balance and should instead report a closed account with a $0 balance.

Paid Before Sent to Collection:
> Loan was paid in full to the lender before the account was sent to collection. Account should have never been sent to collection. Please remove collection from report.

In the Bankruptcy / $0 Balance:
> Account was in the bankruptcy and should show a $0 balance.

Duplicate Account:
> Remove one of the accounts to reflect just one account.

Inaccurate Account Status (Balance, Credit Limit, Past Due, etc):
> Account information such as high credit limit or balance is in accurate.

Incorrect Opening Date:
> Account is not reflecting an opening date or has an inaccurate opening date.

52. Inaccurate Credit Scores

Some risk factors could be inaccurate

One of the greatest concerns of the credit scoring system is the failure of the credit scoring system itself. Scores can be negatively impacted even though there was little chance that the people understood the problem at hand. A misapplication of *risk factors* or *reason codes* may be negatively affecting a credit score. A huge concern is when credit scores are inaccurately calculated.

Brenda first noticed this issue when she was reviewing her credit report with a lender. In the reason codes, a credit score listed "Too many consumer finance companies" (6) below Brenda's credit scores. She had 16 credit references and not one of them was a finance company. She called a customer service representative at the credit bureau and identified the problem. This representative confirmed her suspicion. The credit report did not have a finance company for a current or previous lender. The representative only speculated that one of the accounts was incorrectly listed as a finance company.

In a second instance, the reason code "Lack of recent bank revolving information" (15) appeared under Jen's credit score. She, in fact, had three revolving account balances with her community bank. Two were credit cards and the third was a personal line of credit. Her three lines of credit with the bank was somehow not giving her credit.

Since the credit bureaus only vaguely identify all the factors impacting our scores, we can never fully evaluate the accuracy of our credit scores. The means we can only identify these concerns by asking for the reason codes or risk factors and verify their accuracy. Since the credit bureaus and *Fair Isaac* only release the top four or five factors, we may never be able to fully authenticate our credit scores.

Since the system is a proprietary system, we can only speculate if our credit scores are completely accurate. Since very few of us understand all the factors impacting our scores, our ability is limited. We should take what information is provided with our credit scores and review our credit reports. We need to better understand all the factors that impact credit scores so that we can recognize all the potential issues affecting our credit scores.

53. Duplicate Public Records

◆━━━━━━━━━━━━━━━━━━━━━━━━━━━━━━◆

Review public records section for duplicate references

Each credit report has a *Public Records* section that identifies any recent bankruptcies, judgments, or tax liens. Errors are common in this section with incorrect or duplicate public records especially from judgments and tax liens. Since any number of public records can dramatically effect our scores, we should review this section for accuracy.

Public records influence credit scores for several years from *"Length of time since derogatory public record or collection is too short"* (20), and *"Derogatory public record or collection filed"* (40). They are one of the leading credit score factors that can drop our scores.

There are various reasons for duplicate public records. Public records are generally compiled, processed, and reported to the credit files through less efficient methods. One judgment or tax lien oftentimes shows up as multiple judgments or tax liens. Whatever the circumstance, each additional public record can apply greater pressure on our credit scores.

In order to identify a duplicate public record, we first must recognize the credit agencies in the report. If all three agencies are in a credit report, they will show *XPN (Experian)*, *EQX (Equifax)*, and *TU (Trans Union)* next to each reported account. If a duplicate public record is found, two or more public records will show the identical account coming from the same credit bureau.

If a duplicate judgment or tax lien is discovered, we must dispute that error with the credit bureau and reference the duplicate account. We should send a written letter to the credit bureau to show them the error. Public records are generally more difficult to correct. We may have to dispute the error multiple times before the problem is finally corrected.

Public Record		
Credit Report Date: 1/01/2007		
Judgment	$1,412	Not Satisfied
XYZ Lending	3/04	XPN
Judgment	$1,412	Not Satisfied
XYZ Lending	3/04	XPN
Credit report shows two accounts with the same judgment from Experian (XPN).		

11

Late Payments

Most of us face unexpected financial difficulties in our lives at one time or another. A poor solution is to allow the situation to grow beyond our control or even give up. When facing these financial challenges, we can create a plan and follow some strategies to prevent a credit score free fall. The return to the right road will be quicker and a higher credit score will be the result with an effective plan.

Jack was trying to qualify for a mortgage. He was having difficulty getting his home loan approved. Jack wanted a second mortgage to take some money out from his home for some unexpected medical expenses. Most everyone thought Jack was financially set. However, he was having trouble qualifying for a mortgage because of his credit score. Jack's credit score was 505. There were not a lot of options for second mortgages. In reviewing his credit, Jack had several late payments on a mortgage and other accounts primarily due to a prolonged illness in the family. His credit was absolutely perfect before this unexpected situation occurred.

He sat down with his lender and created a plan to develop several strategies in order to raise his credit score. Jack had some money to pay off some lower balance accounts that had had late payments in the last 12 months. He paid off and closed most of those accounts and then worked to reduce some higher balance credit cards. Within 30 days, his credit score jumped to 558. Within 90 days, it came in at 582. He kept working at it for four straight months and his score kept climbing.

Within a year, his score climbed to the mid 600's. Within 18 months, his credit score climbed to 763. Jack and his lender identified those issues that were greatly affecting his credit score. He reduced their impact and his score increased. He created a winning plan and quickly built his credit score back to a respectable high level.

No one is alone. Many people have faced late payments in their life. Everyone has different financial and credit challenges. Being aware of effective strategies can provide a shorter timeline to reestablish a credit score. We can find light at the end of a shorter tunnel by developing and implementing a plan to restore financial and credit stability. Making correct decisions now can save a lot of future grief for us.

There are ten reason codes that reveal the impact on scores from late payments. Four codes identity the severity of late payments. Two deter-

Determining Impact on Scores

From Late Payments

Factor	Less Impact	More Impact
1. Severity of Late Payments	30 Days Late	Bankruptcy
2. How Recent	Years Ago	Last Month
3. Number of Late Payments	1	Ten
4. Number of Loans with Late Payments	1	Four
5. Loan Balance	$0	$200,000
6. Balance to High Credit Limit Ratio	10%	105%
7. Lender	Bank	Finance Co.
8. Loan Type	Credit Card	Mortgage
9. Length of Account	Five Years	One Month
10. Loan Status	Closed	Open

mine the number of derogatory accounts, one reveals amounts currently past due, and another one identifies large loan balances with late payments. The last two reveal how recent the late payments occurred. These factors can impact our scores for up to seven years. With a Chapter 7 bankruptcy, the influence can be ten years or more. For an unpaid tax lien, its influence can be felt on scores indefinitely.

The severity of late payments has the greatest lasting effect on credit scores. The severity and its influence on scores fall into four categories. These categories identify the level of impact on a credit score, and the length of time the issues impact scores. The four categories are:

Level I	*Spot delinquency.*
Level II	*Serious delinquency.*
Level III	*Severe delinquency.*
Level IV	*Continuous delinquency.*

Spot delinquency is from one or two accounts that maybe have had a recent late payment. Its impact on our scores is felt for upwards of four years. If there are other loans in the file that have a quality payment history, the time to recover is less. We will usually see *"Level of delin-quency on accounts"* (2) as the reason code from spot delinquency.

"Serious delinquency" occurs when there is at least one loan that has had at least two straight months of late payments, has been at least two or more payments behind, or multiple loans in the credit file have had late payments. The time of impact from this level can be felt up to seven years. The warning signs are given by *"Number of accounts with delinquency"* (18) or *"Serious delinquency"* (39).

Severe delinquency comes from a collection, a tax lien, a judgment, a bankruptcy, or when the most of our accounts have had late payments. This type of delinquency impacts scores for up to ten years with one exception. An unpaid tax lien can impact scores indefinitely. *"Too few accounts currently paid as agreed"* (19) and *"Derogatory public re-cord or collection filed"* (40) appears when we reach this level.

Continuous delinquency happens when we have had a *Level III* delin-quency, and then make additional late payments after we have tried to re-establish credit. We have had some past serious derogatory credit issues. We then have reestablished credit and our payments have fallen seriously past due once again. We have demonstrated a complete lack of responsibility. This level of delinquency is described from *"Serious delinquency and derogatory public record or collection filed"* (38). The time of impact can be felt for at least ten or more years.

When we have late payments, we should try to reduce their impact on our scores by limiting their progression The natural progression for late payments starts with one late payment to multiple late payments, finally ending in a collection, a judgment, or a tax lien.

If we can keep to a *Level I* instead of a *Level III* delinquency, the time to recover is less. Allowing loans to fall behind and end up in collection or judgment has a longer negative impact on scores than just one late payment. Limiting the damage by preventing a loan from falling further behind is critical to reestablishing a score. If we do eventually end up in a bankruptcy, with a judgment, a tax lien, or a collection, it is critical that we have no future late payments.

We can never give up. We may face some challenging moments. How-ever, we can recover faster from a devastating situation if we under-stand what we can do. With perseverance and patience, we can build a respected credit score even after the most challenging circumstances. Finding the right strategy and path is critical in saving time and money for each of us facing derogatory credit. A plan and a little direction can produce positive results within months and over the years.

54. Planning & Communication

Create a financial plan to keep loans current

When a financial crisis arises, we are often flooded with problems as the stress of meeting financial obligation builds. Failure to plan and to communicate with the lender usually leads to tougher consequences. One of the best strategies is to develop a financial plan and communicate with each lender when we face the difficulty of meeting current financial obligations.

When we stop communicating with lenders, they have several avenues to seek repayment. They can pull our credit report, contact other creditors, our coworkers, friends, or family. They can send the account to a collection agency or file for judgment. We can go from a *Level I* to a *Level III* delinquency in a relatively short period of time. Running from the problem is not a good solution. At some future time, we will face the consequences of running away from the problem.

We need to go in the right direction. We should review all our outstanding debts, the minimum monthly payments, the future due dates, and the prospective cash flows. A cash flow plan can then be created to better understand our financial situation, meet our monthly obligations and to bring our accounts current.

Once we have created a plan, we should contact each lender to make payment arrangements as outlined. If possible, a helpful customer serviced agent should be located. When that representative is found, we should write down that person's name, employee number, and extension. By working with just one person, we can better communicate and generally have greater success in resolving problems.

We should be reasonable and give ourselves some room in our plan for unexpected expenditures or a shortage of incoming cash flows. Since issues can come up, payment arrangements with creditors should only be made for the short term — 30 to 90 days out. This allows us some room for any future changes.

Most creditors are more willing to work with those people that have created a repayment plan. Having a plan, communicating with the creditors, and following through are all vital to the future success of a plan. A plan can help us bring loans current and helps us rebuild our credit score in a shorter period of time. We can deter some of the negative effects from past due payments, correct our course, and our scores can usually rebound faster with an effective plan.

55. Valuable Loans

Avoid late payments on valuable accounts

As highlighted in the introduction to the chapter, some loans impact credit scores more than others from late payments. The types of loans and lenders, the balances owed, and the length loans are opened are just some of the issues that determine the overall impact on credit scores from late payments. When we identify our more valuable credit references, we need to always keep these loans from being late.

The impact on credit scores from late payment is determined by the number of late payments, the type of loan and lender, how recent the delinquency, the length the account has been open, the balance, an open or closed loan, and the debt or loan balance ratio. *"Level of delinquency on accounts"* (2) can be a factor when we have even one late payment.

One late payment on a mortgage could raise this risk to the highest impacting factor on our score while it may take two or more late payments on a credit card to reach the same impact. If a mortgage or a credit card account has a late payment, the mortgage in most every case impacts credit scores more than the credit card. *"Amount owed on delinquent account"* (33 - EQX / XPN & 31 - TU) appears when we have a late payment on a high balance loan. A late payment on a loan with a higher debt ratio or loan balance ratio drops scores more than a loan with a lower ratio. In addition, a more recent late payment drops a score more than a late payment several years old - *"Time since delinquency is too recent or unknown"* (13).

Higher valued loans should never have a late payment since they can really hurt our score for an extended period of time. Mortgage, an education or auto loan, or an account established for many years are all valuable loans. Since a mortgage or auto loan usually have a higher loan balance, we should avoid having any late payments on these loans. If they have a late payment, they can be difficult to pay off or refinance and will damage our score for years.

We can have greater success and improve our scores faster by keeping our most valued loans from having any late payments. By paying particular attention to our most valued loans, we can be focused in protecting these accounts that really drive our score higher.

56. Containing the Flu

Make an effort to limit any late payments to one loan

The difficulties of maintaining timely payments can be challenging at times when we face a financial crisis. When resources are low and payments are high, we may face decisions about which accounts to pay and which ones to let go. Limiting late payments to one, lesser valued loan can alleviate the damage and help scores recover faster over time.

Dealing with the issue of late payments is similar to having the flu. We want to lessen the number of people with the flu and the severity of the cold. We must minimize the number of accounts with late payments and the severity of late payments.

One 30-day late payment on a loan changes the loan status in our credit report from *'Good standing account'* to a *'Delinquent account'*. This status will remain with the account until the late payment falls from the account, usually in seven years. *Number of accounts with delinquency"* (18) is the warning when multiple loans, open or closed, have at least one late payment. This factor can influence our credit scores for up to seven years.

If most accounts in our credit file have late payments, we could see the factor, *"Too few accounts currently paid as agreed"* (19). This situation arises when the majority of loans in the credit file, whether outstanding or paid in full, have had late payments. We have demonstrated a substantial failure to follow the repayment terms with most of the loans in our credit report.

Any late payment does some damage to credit scores. The question is, *"How much damage?"* Limiting late payments to a one, lower balanced account is preferred since it can be paid off quickly and scores can recover faster. If the account with the late payment is a revolving account, it is best in most instances to close that account after the balance is paid. If we have multiple consecutive late payments, we raise the severity of the late payments, and the total impact and time to recover.

When we have a limited amount of funds, we should first identify those monthly payments that do not report to the credit bureau. Such payments may include those to utilities for phone, gas, or electric. Even if we are 30 or 60 days past due, we usually can retain their services and not have the late payments reported on our credit report. By also limiting any late payments to one lesser valued account, we can reduce the damage to our credit score and *'contain the flu'*.

57. Recent Late Payment

Pay off and close those loans with recent late payments

Most of us will have a late payment at some time in our lifetime. We may have forgotten about a payment or we may have been financially strapped. The impact on a credit score from a recent late payment can be substantial depending on the delinquent account.

First, we should ask these three questions about the account to identify our best strategy:

1. Has the loan been open for at least ten years?
2. Is there only one recent late payment on the account?
3. Is the creditor a non-finance company lender?

If all three questions are 'Yes', we should leave the account open and let time reduce the impact from the late payment. If at least one of the three questions is 'No', we should pay off and close the account in most every situation. If there is a question, we should look at the factors affecting our scores. If *"Level of delinquency on accounts"* (2) is a top factor affecting our scores, we should pay off, transfer the balance, or refinance the delinquent loan to minimize the impact.

The second scenario that could arise is if the account that had the late payment is the only active and open loan in the credit file. With this situation, we would be wise to keep the account open since it would be hard to establish another quality account with such a poor credit rating. We must simply build our score from this one account over time. This will take months and even a year or more.

As previously outlined, recent late payments have a much greater negative impact on scores than those several years old. Recent late payments hurt scores with *"Time since delinquency to recent or unknown"* (13) for several years. Delinquent accounts also drop when there is a higher loan balance versus one that is paid off *"Amount owed on delinquent account"* (34). Last of all, a late payment on a loan 15 year old has less impact on scores than one late payment on a new account.

If a loan has a high balances such as a mortgage or auto loan, we will probably have to wait to build up our score before we can refinance the loan. Otherwise, the interest rate on the new loan may be substantially higher. If we don't have a lot of other issues in the file, it can take several months before the credit score has recovered sufficiently to refinance an auto or mortgage loan and qualify for a low interest rate.

58. Consumer Credit Counseling

Use as a last option before bankruptcy

Consumer credit counseling companies market to everyone that they can lower our interest rate and monthly debt obligations. Even though this is usually true, the effects of consumer credit counseling can potentially be devastating to a credit score. We need to understand the consequences before signing up for their services.

When we sign up to have consumer credit counseling service companies renegotiate a repayment plan, these organizations try to reduce our monthly payments with each of our creditors. Even though they are non-profit, these consumer credit counseling companies are a high revenue industry. Their revenue is generated by taking a certain percentage from our payment. For every $100 in monthly payments the debtor makes, the consumer credit counseling service may retain, for example, $7 from that payment to creditors. Money that could go to debt payoff instead is pocketed by these organizations for their services.

Once a reduced payment plan has been approved by all parties, the lenders may show the account on the credit report as in *"Consumer Credit Counseling"*. Consumer credit counseling can have an effect on our credit in two ways.

First, the payment sent from the consumer credit counseling service to the lender is almost always less than the minimum required payment. Since the payment made to our creditors is less, the account falls behind and late payments can show up continuously until the loan is paid off. We can go from a *Level I* to a *Level III* delinquency in no time. Our credit report appears to have multiple late payments with each loan in consumer credit counseling. The effect in many cases is quite severe and impacts scores for years.

Second, even if all the late payments on the accounts are never reported, the consumer credit counseling service can still jeopardize our future loan qualifications for years to come. By having just one current or past loan reflect *"Consumer credit counseling"*, many lenders consider this account as part of a bankruptcy and will deny any future credit application.

We should not be lured into these program without understanding future implications to our credit and our scores. We should use this program as a last resort to keep ourselves out of bankruptcy.

59. Debt Consolidation Companies

Damage to credit can be unexpectedly severe

Debt consolidation companies promote *"One payment pays all plan"* that can reduce the pressure of maintaining an overburdening debt load. Their clients can send in one payment to a debt consolidation company. That company then sends the monthly payments to each creditor. Although their intentions may be sincere, their actions can still negatively impact our credit score.

A debt consolidation company is not considered a consumer credit counseling company. Nevertheless, it has a similar promotion to consumer credit counseling services; *"You make one payment to us, and we will pay all your bills."* or *"We will reduce your interest by thousands of dollars."* We want someone to ease the burden of tracking our monthly bills and making our monthly payments.

The problems from these programs can be two-fold. First, our creditors can see a third-party check is paying our monthly debts. From a lender's view point, debt consolidation companies are similar to consumer credit counseling services. At times, creditors cannot differentiate between the two and change the account status to, *"Consumer credit counseling"*. This statement affects our stellar credit rating. Unfortunately, this does happen and the results are devastating. Debt consolidation companies are not credit experts, just good salesmen trying to make money.

The second concern has left many people high and dry. Once the funds have been received from the debtors, some companies have failed to pay the funds to the client's creditors in a timely manner. Their credit report subsequently reflects late payments. Our credit can quickly go from a *Level I,* to a *Level II*, and potentially arrive to a *Level III* delinquency in no time. This scenario has played out many times and has devastated many credit scores. Adding insult to injury, the money can disappear and the victims could potentially pay the same debt twice.

We should be aware of the dangers that could potentially affect our credit scores before signing up for their debt consolidation services. Our credit scores and any future consideration for loan approval could potentially be affected by following their program.

60. Moving

◆━━◆

Communicate with creditors, utilities, and other accounts

We, as Americans, tend to move to a new homes more so than in times past. We are promoted, transferred, or move up to a better home. We must quickly update our mailing address with each creditor, utility and any other open account. Too often, we fail to properly communicate with these entities and outstanding bills are returned to senders unpaid, and accounts fall delinquent.

A person moves and fails to properly communicate with lenders and utilities. Even though a change-of-address card may be submitted at the post office, it is not a catch-all for all our personal mail. Even if the change-of-address card does forward our mail, there is no guarantee that our mail will be forwarded. Some mail may never arrive at the new address because it is up to the postal carrier to forward our mail and they are not 100% reliable. Many bills may be mailed to our old address and may never arrive to their forwarded destination.

As a result, loan payments can be late, past utility or medical bills may be left unpaid because they have never arrive to our new home. The end result can be late payments on outstanding loans and even collections on utility and medical bills. We may never even know about such bills until we apply for credit and discover the damage on our credit.

There are several steps we should follow to ensure that we make a smooth transition to avoid any misunderstandings. First, we should contact all our of creditors, utilities, and medical providers by both phone and in writing to notify them of our new address. Second, we should complete a change of address card. Last, we should try to prepay our loans a month or two in advance if we have the resources. We often are so distracted when we move that we forget about our monthly debts.

It doesn't take much time to have a late payment or even a collection show up on our credit report. It is our responsibility to communicate with the our lenders and creditors when we move, not their responsibility to find us. We must take preventative action before we move to protect our credit rating and score. By taking such small actions, we can prevent a miscommunication which can cost us our respected score.

61. Seriously Past Due

◆───────────────────────────────────◆

Payoff loans that have been seriously past due

Most of us when we have a late payment on an outstanding balance don't realize the potential damage we can do to our credit score if we let the account continue to remain behind. We must recognize the terms of a seriously past due account since the damage to our scores can be substantial and long lasting.

There are two definitions of seriously past due. A seriously past due account is at least one loan in the credit report that shows at least two payments past due at any one time, or has had at least two consecutive payments late. These late payments can be several years old and even paid off, and still impact have a substantial downward impact on our scores. They can be from an account that simply fell behind several payments. Its damage is extensive and we should avoid such scenarios.

"Serious delinquency", (39) is the warning sign when we have a loan that has been seriously past due. If we have a loan with seriously late payments, we really only have one real strategy to limit its damage. We should pay off and close the account. By transferring the remaining balance or refinancing the loan, we can help our score recover. We simply need to remove this outstanding loan from our credit record. It is best we start now, by paying it off and closing it. Nevertheless, its impact can be felt for seven years until the seriously past due payments fall from the credit record.

In the given example, the SRS credit card had payments that fell behind as late as 150 days behind. The UVS credit card had two consecutive late payments. Both situations are consider, *'Seriously delinquent'*. The only option is to payoff and close both accounts. The faster a loan can be paid off and closed, the quicker our scores can recover.

Payment History

Credit Report Date: 1/01/2007

Creditor	**Balance**	**Payment History**
SRS Credit Card	*$515*	*111154321111 (5 - 9/06)* *111111111111*
UVS Credit Card	*$211*	*111221111111 (2 - 10/06)* *111111111111*

1 means current payments, a 2 signals a 30 day late payment, a 3 was 60 days late, 4 was 90 days, and 5 was 120 days late. Both loans in this example should be paid off and closed.

---

62. Divorce

Identify all our joint liabilities while going through in a divorce

With countless marriages ending in divorce, many of us will face or have faced the stress of separation and the impending liability. Even though a divorce court usually separates the debt responsibilities for each party, the liability from the creditor remains to each responsible party signed to that loan.

A divorce is truly not final until all the joint liabilities are paid and closed. Many mistakenly believe that once a divorce court has ruled on the separation of debts, that they are no longer responsible for those obligations assigned to the ex-spouse. Divorce court simply divides the liabilities and assets between the two parties. Regardless of what the divorce court has ruled, all parties are still liable in most cases for those joint debts. Letting those debts go could jeopardize our credit scores.

Lenders simply report the responsible party's information from any loan to the credit report. Those parties which have signed on the loan have the payment history reported to their credit report. Unless a court of law declares that a creditor must remove a certain person from an account, the loan information continues to report until the loan is paid off and closed. We may be divorced and the court require our ex-spouse to pay the bill. Even so, the payment history from each joint liability will continue to report on each person's credit file.

When working through a separation and divorce, we must identify all our debts, including personal loans. If there is any question, we should pull our credit report or call each creditors to identify all the joint loans. Lenders should be contacted and they may even require the divorce papers to show the responsibility of the debt payments. We should request that the lenders notify us in the event an account is on the verge of reporting a late payment.

When negotiations are finalizing the divorce, particular attention should be given to joint liabilities. Parties seeking divorce who have joint debts should have a repayment plan approved between the parties until the loan is paid off. Once the debt is paid, the account should be closed from any future borrowing activity.

By taking these preventive actions, we can possibly alleviate the problems from joint liabilities in a divorce. Misunderstandings can be avoided which can drop both parties' credit scores.

63. Alimony and Child Support

◆━━━━━━━━━━━━━━━━━━━━━━━━━━━━━━━━━━━━━━◆

Past due child support payments can impact scores for years

Those people who end up in a divorce must not only pay attention to joint liabilities, but also to alimony and to child support payments. Failure to pay timely support payments can result in collections and judgments from a government agency. Since alimony and child support is ongoing, past due collections or judgments can affect scores for years.

Government agencies try various aggressive methods to collect alimony and child support to alleviate the taxpayer's burden from providing welfare to the ex-spouse and raising the children. When we fall behind on these support payments, the government agency files for collection or judgment to collect the past due amount. With a collection, the account can be ongoing until we bring the child support current. The collection remains in the file for another seven years after being paid. With a judgment, the entity enforcing the child support payments can garnish wages or go after real property to make up past due payments. Either way, their actions can be devastating to credit scores.

The first concern for those making child support payments is to always make timely payments. If a financial crisis arises, we should contact the government agency or the court to ask for temporary relief. Communication is extremely vital to maintain a positive credit rating. If we fall behind and fail to respond to their requests for payment, the consequences can be severe when the account is sent for collection. We can go from a perfect credit rating to a *Level III* delinquency in no time. *"Derogatory public record or collection filed"* (40) is the road sign that appears and our score is severely impacted.

A fraudulent claim of past due child support pursued by an ex-spouse can also cause havoc. The government agency simply sends a request for an appearance and the spouse may never received it. Due to non-appearance, a judgment may be issued and is not discovered until a credit report is pulled. Even after documenting all child support payments and having the claim deemed fraudulent, it still can be difficult removing the judgment from the credit report.

There are two strategies to follow to protect our credit. We should always provide correct contact information to the government agency. Finally, we should always make timely payments to avoid the devastating impact from any collections or judgments they can file.

64. Boat and Oar Rule

Recover faster from late payments

A big mistake we can make when facing financial challenges is to, *"Let everything go!"* The time to recover takes longer and the road to improvement more difficult. A wise strategy to rebuild a credit score is to identify at least one quality loan and maintain timely payments throughout any financial challenge. It is like having a life raft available in the middle of the ocean. It is better to have one, than be left without.

We may lose a job, have a death in the family, or face a serious medical crisis. A financial challenge can be never ending as problems build. Monthly payments on utilities and monthly payments pushed back can eventually reflect on our credit report. We may fall behind on credit cards, auto, and even mortgage loans. Managing the finances along with the personal stress from the situation is challenging. It is like being in the middle of the ocean with no raft or paddle to return to shore. Daily life must continue, however, because life doesn't stop. We must identify strategies to navigate the financial crisis.

When faced with such situations, we can make a very poor decision by letting every debt fall behind. Many people can attest from similar situations that the price to pay after a total collapse is almost never ending. It is like we end up drowning without ever trying to return to shore.

When facing the prospects of reduction in income or higher expenses, we should rank the quality each loan brings to our credit score. The highest value loan is one account that should remain open and active throughout the crisis until credit can be reestablished and the crisis has passed. This loan should be kept current throughout the financial challenge. It is the life raft that will help us return to shore must faster.

If we can keep additional loans current, we should identify the next most valuable loan. Each additional loan that is kept current is like an extra oar that can be used to return much faster to shore. The more oars in the water, the faster we return to shore, or in this case, the quicker we can build our credit score. Keeping the greatest number of loans current is important.

Even this one loan can be a lifesaver and help us to reestablish a credit score more quickly. Without it, we can spin in the rough waters going in no real direction. It is a strategy that is very effective in reestablishing a credit score. Once the crisis is over, our scores will have a better foundation to build in the future.

65. Home Foreclosure

◆━━◆

Mortgage late payments affect a score for years

When payments fall behind on any account in our file, a mortgage can create additional damage to our scores with a *"Foreclosure"* notice placed on the account. The multiple late payments and foreclosure both create derogatory marks. A foreclosure is like a extra weight that can hold credit scores down for years.

There are two issues from a home foreclosure that can affect our credit rating. First, the multiple late payments from a home mortgage create a substantial drag on credit scores. Second, the status of foreclosure on any account in the file is a substantial derogatory mark.

A home foreclosure is the process of a lender to repossess the property from the borrowers. A mortgage can be placed into foreclosure even with one 30-day late payment. In most circumstances, lenders wait until the mortgage is at least three payments past due before starting the foreclosure process. Lenders may place the mortgage in foreclosure and still give time to the homeowner to bring the loan current. Lenders usually want the full amount brought current before they will take the loan out of foreclosure. However, the damage is done to the credit bureau.

The impact on credit scores can be profound. Any mortgage late usually raises the impact on our credit scores from *"Level of delinquency on accounts"* (2). Multiple late payments from a mortgage not only raise the level of negative impact from *"Seriously past due"* (39), it also impacts our score with *"Amount owed on delinquent account"* (34 - EQX / XPN & 31 - TU. Many months may pass before the loan is brought current or the home is repossessed. The delinquency and its impact on our scores may to continue to build with each month.

A lender must be given written notice in most instances before a loan can be placed into foreclosure. Once the mortgage has been placed in foreclosure, the credit file displays, *"Foreclosure"* next to the account. This account status gives the loan a serious derogatory rating. Even if the loan is subsequently brought current, the foreclosure status will remain on the account for seven years. Many loan approval systems will deny a loan simply because of a foreclosure in the file.

Since a mortgage is a highly valued loan, we need to keep this loan current and avoid any possibility of foreclosure. The cost will be substantially more in the future with a foreclosure. This loan should be one of the last accounts to fall delinquent when we face a financial crisis.

66. Negotiating a Settlement

Better to be 'Satisfied' than to be 'Settled'

When a loan or collection is overdue, or the original loan payments cannot be met, we may try to reach an agreement an agreement with the lender to payoff the account. When we negotiate such an agreement, we should understand the differences between a *'Satisfied'* versus a *'Settled'* account and how they each can affect our scores.

A common mistake with past due accounts or unusually large balances is when we negotiate a settlement. We come to terms with a creditor that is different from the original agreement. Failing to properly negotiate this account can drop our credit score even more. The issue centers around the wording in the agreement. A *settled account* is derogatory while a *satisfied account* is viewed more positively.

A settled account means that we have come to a negotiated settlement with the lender that is less than the original repayment terms of the loan. Once a settlement has been reached, the creditor usually updates the loan and places *'Account settled'* next to the loan in the credit report. Such a reference in a credit file is a bad mark. This term implies that the full terms of the loan were not met by the debtor. Since the loan is updated, it is like having a recent late payment.

When negotiating a reduced payment amount, we need to reach an agreement with the creditor that reflects the account as *'Paid in full'* or *'Satisfied'*. Either of these terms mean that the original loan terms have been met by the debtor. This action reflects more positively on a credit report than a *settled account*. The creditor may still reach an agreement with the borrower that is a less than full repayment, and classify the loan as *'Satisfied'*.

When a negotiated settlement has been reached, we should ask the creditor for a copy of the proposed agreement before sending the money. We can then confirm that the creditor is listing the loan as *'Satisfied'* rather than *'Settled'* before we send them the money. Once the payment has been sent, we should ask for a letter certified from the company that the account has been *'Paid in full'* or *'Satisfied.'* Once we receive the written receipt, we should then forward a copy over to the credit bureaus so that they can update the account information in our credit report. When we understand the different terms, we can protect ourselves from having another bad mark that can hurt our scores.

67. Collections

Creditors have seven years to collect the debt

Creditors send past due accounts to collection agencies as a means to recover monies that are still owed. These collection companies then file notices with the credit bureaus to attain greater visibility on a past due amount. Since collections are considered severe delinquency, we should keep every account from progressing to this level.

A collection is found in the payment history of a credit report. The creditor listed is known as a collection company and the account generally shows *"Collection"* with the account. *"Length of time since derogatory public record or collection is too short"* (20) and *"Derogatory public record or collection filed"* (40) can both have a substantial downward effect on credit scores. Similar to a judgment or tax lien, collections can cause considerable damage.

An account usually does not go to a collection company until the loan payments are at least six months or more past due. Therefore, we should not run from creditors, but rather find a workable solution. We have some time to find a suitable repayment plan before creditors send the account to a collection company. Lenders often accept smaller payments in lieu of a collection agency as long as the loan is being repaid.

Collection agencies have seven years from the servicing date or the date the account went to a collection, or from the last payment activity to collect the debt. If the collection is older than seven years, the debt can no longer be collected. We should first ask the collection agency to identify the collection's servicing date. Every agency must provide us with this date upon our request, even if the collection is sold to a second collection agency. When it is sold, the servicing date remains the same.

If a debt goes to collection, we should pay off the debt as soon as possible to limit its impact. When collections are paid, a written receipt should be requested and kept for at least seven years since these accounts are often sold and can appear as a second collection. With a receipt, we can protect ourselves from having to pay the collection again.

Sometimes the collection account remains on the credit report indefinitely. If we have such a collection, we can submit a dispute letter to remove the collection from our credit file after seven years from the servicing date (if unpaid), or seven years after the account was paid. We should recognize when this derogatory account should drop off our report so that it doesn't impact our scores beyond industry guidelines.

68. Old Collections

Our scores can be impacted a second time

When we identify an older collection with an outstanding balance, paying off the collection may update the derogatory mark and drop our scores again. We should understand their effect on our scores when we work with older collections to avoid impacting them a second time.

There are two primary problems with older collections. The first problem occurs when a collection is paid. Collection agencies do not always report on a timely or regular basis to the credit reports. These companies report a collection on a credit report and then wait to be paid. Once paid, the agency should report a $0 balance within 90 days. However, collection agencies often take months or even years, and sometimes never show the account as paid. They can continue to report a balance and a past due amount which both continue to drop our scores.

The second concern is updating an old collection. When the collection is finally reported as paid, the effect on scores is similar to a brand new collection being reported to the credit report. The account is updated and the *Last Active Date* reflects a recent month and year. *"Length of time since derogatory public record or collection is too short"* (20) can reappear as a major concern with our scores. Such collections impact scores once when they are first reported, and a second time when they are paid. They remain on our report for seven years after being paid.

Since credit scores are greatly influenced by the payment activity in the last 24 months, an updated derogatory mark can negatively affect scores a second time. If we have an older collection, we should try to negotiate an agreement in which the collection agency agrees to remove the mark from our file upon payment. Removing the account would avoid having the credit scores from being impacted twice by the same collection.

Payment History

Credit Report Date: 1/01/2007

Creditor	Last Active	Balance
Before		
ADH Collection	6/03	$412
After		
ADH Collection	1/07	$0

The collection is paid and the account is updated to show $0 balance on the report.

69. Tax Liens

Unpaid tax liens can remain indefinitely

Those who have past due taxes are advised to resolve the problem with the government agency as quick as possible. Unpaid tax bills can often lead to a lien and report to a credit report. These liens will remain on the report indefinitely and will dramatically impact our scores. Since tax liens are classified as a *Level III* delinquency, we should resolve this matter before a lien is filed with the local court to avoid its negative effect on scores.

Unlike collections, judgments, or bankruptcies, an unpaid tax lien has a life of its own. Once the taxes are paid in full, the lien remains on the credit report seven years from the date the lien was paid. The credit risk on scores is felt from, *"Derogatory public record or collection filed"* (40). If left unpaid, this one factor can influence credit scores for years without end.

When there is a past due tax bill, we should always try to establish communication with the appropriate government agency whether local, state or federal to resolve the issue. To the surprise of many, the Internal Revenue Service even has a Taxpayer Advocate's office that is responsible in resolving tax issues between taxpayers and the I.R.S. We can thereby avoid working with multiple representatives who are unfamiliar with our particular situation.

A tax lien often reflects as duplicate liens or can also show unpaid when in fact, they have been paid. In addition, tax liens also remain on a credit report even if a determination is made by the appropriate government agency that there was no unpaid tax bill. If we for example fail to respond to a past due tax bill and a lien was filed, the lien will remain. We must always pay attention to any past due tax bills and take immediate action against them to limit their potential impact on our scores.

Public Record

Credit Report Date: 1/01/2007

Before
Tax Lien   Reported 06/03   Amount - 519
                                                  Last Active 06/03

- -

After
Tax Lien Satisfied   Reported 06/03   Amount - 519
                                                  Last Active 12/06

Tax lien was filed in June 2003 and paid December 2006. Will drop from report December 2013.

70. Judgments

The effect can punish our credit score

Like collections and tax liens, judgments are a *Level III* delinquency and are one of the greatest derogatory marks we can have on a credit score. A judgment is reported to a credit file when we have either failed to respond to a court summons on a civil case, or lose a criminal case and a fine is posed. We should make every effort to avoid a judgment because of its damage to our scores lasts for years.

When other forms of collecting a past due account have failed, lenders resort to judgments as a means for repayment on a past due account. Lenders file a claim in court after efforts to collect a debt have been unsuccessful. When a trial is heard and a judgment is issued by the court against a defendant, the creditor has additional opportunities to collect the debt. Plaintiffs can garnish wages or secure liens on real estate in hopes of being repaid. A judgment appears on the public record of our credit report. *"Derogatory public record or collection filed"* (40) is the sign that appears following a judgment.

Once a judgment has been awarded by the court, the creditor has seven years to collect the debt. A judgment impacts a score for those seven years even if the amount is eventually paid. The more recent, the larger the number of judgments, or an unpaid judgment have a greater impact on our scores.

When we face a summons to appear in court, we should try to resolve the matter before the court proceeding. If a judgment is awarded against us, we should then try and payoff the judgment. Since judgments are not updated monthly, a satisfaction letter should be requested and a copy sent to the courthouse and the credit bureaus so that the respective entities can be update their records. We should request a credit report a few months later to ensure the judgment shows paid.

Public Record		
Credit Report Date: 1/01/2007		
Before		
Judgment	Filed 02/04	Amount - 912
After		
Judgment Satisfied	Filed 02/04	Amount - 912
		Last Active 12/04
Judgment was filed in February 2004 and was paid and satisfied in December 2004.		

71. Chapter 13 Bankruptcy

◆━━━━━━━━━━━━━━━━━━━━━━━━━━━━━━━━━━━━◆

Maintain timely payments on at least one loan

A Chapter 13 bankruptcy occurs when we seek debt relief from a bankruptcy court. A repayment plan is then organized and approved by the court. Repayment can take up to five years to pay owing creditors. Since this bankruptcy remains on a credit report for seven years after it is filed, it is considered a *Level III* delinquency.

In a Chapter 13 bankruptcy, the court takes our debts, creates, and approves a repayment plan for each lender. The amount repaid is usually less than the minimum monthly payment, causing multiple late payments to be reported on those loans. Some secured debts such as home or auto may be excluded in the bankruptcy. Since those in a Chapter 13 bankruptcy are warned not to take out new debts, they may have limited opportunities to build credit while making repayments.

The impact on credit scores is felt for many years from the factor, *"Derogatory public record or collection filed"* (40). Since the bankruptcy can take years to complete, we should have some active on-time accounts before entering this bankruptcy instead of waiting until the plan is paid. If we wait, it could take many years to rebuild a score.

While in a Chapter 13 bankruptcy, we will have limited opportunities to rebuild a credit score. It is therefore critical that we have at least one loan outside the bankruptcy to rebuild the credit score. This one account should have timely payments made before, during, and after the bankruptcy to build the credit score. Having at least one positive payment history is an important step to rebuilding a credit score.

By maintaining timely payments on at least one quality loan, we can rebuild our credit score faster in a shorter period of time after the bankruptcy plan has been completed.

Public Record		
Credit Report Date: 1/01/2007		
Before		
Chapter 13 Bankruptcy	Filed 05/01	
After		
Chapter 13 Bankruptcy	Filed 05/01	Discharged - 06/05
Chapter 13 Bankruptcy was filed in March 2001 and was discharged in June 2005.		

72. Chapter 7 Bankruptcy

Maintain one loan to reduce its effect on scores

A Chapter 7 bankruptcy is the greatest single event that can drop our credit scores the most. This bankruptcy's influences credit scores for up to ten years after the filing date. Similar to a Chapter 13 bankruptcy, a Chapter 7 bankruptcy is considered a *Level III* delinquency. Those who have recently filed or are in the process of filing a Chapter 7 bankruptcy should plan now to recover from its damaging impact on scores.

A Chapter 7 bankruptcy is a liquidation of unsecured assets and a renegotiation of some secured assets. Attorneys often advise clients to throw every loan into the bankruptcy. This can be poor financial advise for our scores. We must plan now to develop quality credit and offset he bankruptcy's punishing effects on our score. The quicker we act, the faster we can rebuild our credit score.

The reason codes, *"Derogatory public record or collection filed"* (40) and *"Time since derogatory public record or collection is too short"* (20) appear with the credit scores after filing a Chapter 7 bankruptcy. Even if the bankruptcy is dismissed, the effects on the credit score still remain for ten years after the filing date. This bankruptcy should only be used as a last choice when all other options have failed because of its long-term impact on scores.

Don't procrastinate to rebuild the credit! Rebuilding a credit score from rock bottom is always more challenging than when we have at least one ongoing quality credit reference. We should try to re-establish a credit score by leaving out at least one quality loan. Such possible loans include a credit card, overdraft account, or a mortgage. A score can then increase much quicker when timely payments are made until additional quality credit references can be established after the bankruptcy. If we have more accounts that are in good standing during the bankruptcy, our scores have more resources in which to recover quicker.

Public Record

Credit Report Date: 1/01/2007

Before
Chapter 7 Bankruptcy   Filed   7/03

- -

After
Chapter 7 Bankruptcy   Filed   7/03   Discharged - 10/03

Chapter 7 Bankruptcy was filed in July 2003 and discharged in October 2003.

73. Public Record and Seriously Past Due

Avoid future late payments after a public record or collection

The combination of factors that have the greatest negative effect on a credit score is a public record or collection, and subsequent late payments that are seriously past due. This combination's influence on scores is even more devastating than a single event such as a bankruptcy. It becomes additionally difficult to build our credit score. Those who have a public record or collection must avoid future late payments since it is considered a *Level IV* or *continuous delinquency*.

If we fall seriously past due on loan payments after a collection or a public record, the credit scores are affected by *"Serious delinquency and derogatory public record or collection filed"* (38). It is a big warning sign that appears and affects our scores for years. Such borrowers have demonstrated a true lack of credit responsibility. It is like being placed in solitary confinement and is properly called the, *'Black Hole'*.

The credit scoring system identifies a single event such as a bankruptcy, judgment, tax lien, or collection shows up on our credit report. *"Derogatory public record or collection filed"* (40) is the road sign that appears after a single event. It can continually impact our credit scores so that we cannot rebuild them. If we continue to demonstrate a lack of responsibility and have additional late payments, we face even more challenges and time to rebuild our score. It could take several more years to build a respectable credit score.

Once late payments have been made after a bankruptcy, tax lien, judgment, or collection, this credit risk will usually be the top factor impacting credit scores for several years. We cannot just remove it. We should never go down this path. It is not worth it. Once we have a public record or collection, it is extremely critical that we maintain timely payments on every future loan. Failure to do so could cost us a lot of money. That is, if loan approval is even possible.

Public Record

Credit Report Date: 1/01/2007

Judgment   Filed   02/04   Amount—912

Creditor	**Reporting Date**	**Balance**	**Payment History**
WXW Credit Card	6/06	$1,412	112221111111 (2 - 10/06) 111111111111

Judgment was filed in February 2004 and a late payment occurred in April 2006 on credit card.

74. Credit Repair Companies

They are costly and can cause more harm than good

Credit repair companies are high pressure firms that over-promise and under-deliver. They usually charge high up-front fees and promise to fix our credit. Some even cite possible loopholes in the law that can force creditors to remove bad ratings from our credit report. We can do a lot on our own with similar results and save ourselves hundreds if not thousands of dollars by understanding our rights and the system.

These credit repair companies often cite laws claiming that if the creditor doesn't *"have this"* or *"do that"*, the bad mark must be removed. The Federal Trade Commission along with several other state regulators have warned time and again that these loop holes in the law do not exist. *"When it comes to credit repair, only time, a conscientious effort, and a personal debt repayment plan will improve your credit report. No credit repair company or consumer has the right to remove accurate, correct information from a credit report,"* stated Brad Elbein from the Federal Trade Commission.

No one should ever base the hope of removing a bad mark on a credit report in a loophole in the law that doesn't exist. Some people claim that they have had their credit fixed through such loopholes using the services of these experts. Many people have spent a substantial amount of money to have their credit fixed with no real results. In most cases, these individuals have been duped. The credit repair industry has a troubled reputation of failing to deliver what they promised.

Even if a bad mark has been removed through the efforts of a credit repair company, there is no guarantee that that mark will stay off our credit report. Sometimes the creditor reports the derogatory mark once again to the credit report even after an the credit repair companies' dispute. Since we have no proof in writing from the creditor to remove the bad mark, it can still reappear. We may be left with the same derogatory rating and a lot less money.

If we have tried to correct an inaccuracy or other problem on our credit report with no real results, a credit repair company or an attorney who specializes in the *Fair Credit Reporting Act* in this instance may be able to provide a valued service. Before enlisting their help, we should ask for recommendations from past clients, avoid paying for counseling services up front, and have an agreement signed detailing the services the company plans to provide.

12

Danger Zone

James was a doctor who had just finished medical school and was starting his residency at a local hospital. Even though he had over $100,000 in student loans, he maintained a 763 credit score and qualified for a loan on a house. His problems didn't start with the purchase of the house, it started after he purchased the house.

Within two months of purchasing the house, James and his wife wanted to finish the basement. He had started some work on it, but he wanted to take out a home equity loan to finish the job. His newly constructed home was appreciating nicely and the equity was sufficient to take out a $25,000 loan. However, he had done two things that affected his ability to qualify for the home equity loan.

James had opened up a bank credit card with a national bank and a merchant credit card with a home furnishings company. He had balances that were about 75% of the credit limits. His credit scores dropped from 763 to 668 within four months because of these two accounts. The combination of risks (multiple open accounts, high balances, and types of accounts) had dropped his scores almost 100 points. He had no idea.

He jumped into action and created a plan to quickly reestablish his credit score. He quickly went to the creditors and paid off the entire balances and closed the accounts. Within 35 days, his credit scores jumped to 757. He had made quick strategies and implemented the plan, and his scores rebounded. Within the following month, he had secured the money for his home equity loan and finish his basement.

We should stay away from these areas of concern. When a combination of credit risk increases, the credit scores are impacted even more. These areas of concern can be like large potholes. Once fallen into, we will find that these potholes are large and can extremely difficult to climb out from them.

The concerns arise when a one loan or a combination of loans impact credit scores from several risk factors. For example, opening one loan adds risk and negatively affects a score. Open multiple loans within a month or two compounds the risk. The type of loans determines the eventual impact on our scores. Multiple consumer loans have more negative impact on our scores than multiple education loans.

The impact to credit scores may be 100 points or more depending on the combined risks. These combinations can happen to practically anyone. Many people have found themselves going down this road. The greatest reason for being down this road is a lack of understanding of the credit scoring system.

Even though some of these combinations may have been briefly covered in prior chapters, they are too important without further explanation. We should identify all these areas of risk and be familiar enough with them to stay away. Once we enter and proceed down this path, the road back can be extremely difficult. Credit scores can drop fast and we may have limited options to rebuild them. We should use extreme caution and avoid going into any of the following areas. The road signs can be attractive to enter, but they are deceptive. Once inside, it is extremely difficult to exit. It is better to recognize the warning signs before we enter, then after we are trapped. Education and recognition is a big key in avoiding these lonely roads.

75. Combinations of Risk

Recognize combinations that can our impact scores

We have identified several credit risk factors that can affect our scores. Combination of credit risk can be additionally detrimental to credit scores. When these layers of risks are combined, they can dramatically affect scores. Identifying these factors and understanding how layers of credit risk factors affect scores is critical to avoiding these pitfalls.

There are five primary credit issues that increase the level of our credit risk. They include the following:

1. Late Payments
2. New Loans
3. High Debt or Loan Balance Ratios
4. Number and Type of Outstanding Loan Balances
5. Number and Type of Lenders

Any combination of these factors increase the level of personal credit risk and lower our credit scores even more. A credit score can suddenly drop a 100 points or more within a month or two with multiple combinations. Many of us may find ourselves in these areas without realizing what has happened until it is too late. The fall can be short, swift, and untimely. The climb out can be extremely difficult. Whatever the combinations, the effect on credit scores can be unduly harsh.

A person for example has a newly established revolving loan with a debt ratio at 100%. If a late payment is made on that loan, the effect on the credit scores is much more than a late payment on a ten year old credit card with a debt ratio below 20%. The number of combined credit risk factors determines the ultimate impact on scores.

If we really want to drop our scores, we should file a Chapter 7 bankruptcy against all our current debts. After the bankruptcy, we establish numerous new loans with a finance company. We run up the debt ratios past 100% and never make a payment. We let the accounts fall seriously past due. We will then reach credit futility in no time.

If we don't want to go this route, we must first identify all the credit risk factors and any combinations that can really affect credit scores. Once identified, we should avoid these multiple risk factors. By recognizing and making efforts to avoid added risks, we can find greater success improving our credit scores by avoiding any sudden surprises.

76. High Ratios on Multiple Loans

Avoid multiple loan balances that exceed their credit limits

We sometimes run up the balances on our credit cards and other personal lines of credit unaware of what amount we still have available. Eventually, we may even exceed the credit limits on those revolving accounts. When multiple revolving balances have exceeded their credit limits, credit scores drop substantially.

Credit scores are affected when even one revolving loan balance exceeds 50% of its credit limit. The risk increases when multiple revolving accounts exceed 50% of their credit limit ratio. The more loans, the greater the impact on credit scores.

As both the balance to high credit limit or debt ratio increases along with the number of outstanding accounts, the level of credit risk continues to rise. When multiple revolving loans exceed their high credit limits, credit scores drop from *"Amount owed on accounts too high"* (1) or *"Proportion of balances to credit limits too high on revolving accounts"* (10). Depending on the number of accounts, the payment history, and the types of lender, our scores can drop 100 points or more when multiple accounts have high debt ratios exceeding 100%.

Since credit scores can drop to lower levels, consolidating by refinancing the debts with a new loan is unlikely. The only real solution to the problem is to pay down the balances. By avoiding this dangerous credit risk, we can avoid having a low credit score for a lengthy period of time. Don't let multiple balances exceed 50% of the limit and especially 100% of the credit limit. It's a sure path to a credit score wreck.

Payment History

Creditor	Credit Limit	Balance	Ratio
Before			
VFS Credit Card	$1000	$1112	111%
DST Home Equity Loan	$10,000	$10,100	101%
After			
VFS Credit Card	$1000	$450	45%
DST Home Equity Loan	$10,000	$4,800	48%

Balances are paid down on revolving loans to balances below 50% of the credit limits.

77. Open Multiple Loans

Avoid opening multiple loans within a year

When we open multiple loans within a short period of time, each new loan adds to our level of credit risk. The greater the number of new loans, the greater the risk and lower the score. This risk increases when we borrow against these new accounts — especially revolving loans. Therefore, we should limit the number of new loans each year.

When we buy a new home, car, or other large item, we usually finance the purchase. Additional accessories are often purchased and are usually financed by opening additional consumer loans. The more loans opened over a shorter period of time, the greater the drop with our credit scores. Our level of credit risk increases from *"Too many accounts recently opened"* (9).

The amount of impact is dependent on the types of loans and the amount borrowed. Consumers loans, large balances, and high debt and loan balance ratios can all combine to knock down our scores. When credit is utilized on these new loans, the level of risk is even higher. It is these loans we must pay particular attention to space out. New education and mortgage loans have less impact on our scores than consumer loans. We are wise to limit new accounts especially consumer loans to no more than one per year when we have an established credit file.

If we want to finance additional items, we should utilize current outstanding, low balance, revolving lines of credit. If we have discovered this problem after opening multiple loans, the best solution is to pay off and close these loans. This action reduces the level of credit risk and should raise the credit score to levels before we took out the new loans.

Payment History

Credit Report Date: 1/01/2007

Creditor	Opening Date	Balance	Limit
Before			
DRS Credit Card	10/06	$728	$1,500
DGI Home Equity Loan	11/06	$8,141	$10,000
ABC Bank	10/06	$560	$1,000
After			
DRS Credit Card	10/06	$0	Account Closed
DGI Home Equity Loan	11/06	$4,800	$10,000
ABC Bank	10/06	$0	Account Closed

Three loans opened in the last three months. Two loans are subsequently paid off and closed.

78. Multiple Loans with Finance Companies

Avoid easy cash loan offers

Having loans with quality lenders is an important factor for higher credit scores. When we open a loan with a high risk lender, the credit scores are negatively impacted. When we take out additional loans with these types of lenders, the credit scores can drop even more.

Finance companies and payday lenders market themselves as a quick cash lender. Applicants do not have to wait long to obtain their needed cash. Finance companies market themselves primarily to retailers who use their financing options for their customers. They offer 90 day, 180 day, and one year same-as-cash options to merchants so that both the merchants and the finance companies can expand their customer base. Payday lenders on the other hand market themselves directly to us as a quick cash lender. We can take out a loan within minutes of application as long as we have employment.

Once we have established the first loan, these lenders try to sell us additional loan products. They may offer us auto loans, home equity loans, or other personal lines of credit. These lenders even may solicit us with checks in the mail or other pre-approved loans. When multiple loans are opened from these lenders, the impact from *"Too many consumer finance accounts"* (6) continues to grow and negatively impacts our credit scores with each additional loan.

We should avoid these companies if at all possible. We should never use them for personal, auto, or home equity loans. If we have a current loan, we should it pay off as soon as possible and request no more solicitation. Building a quality score means using quality lenders. If we want an 800 credit score, we should steer clear of these companies.

Payment History

Creditor	Credit Limit	Balance
Before		
GHI Finance	$1000	$750
JKL Finance Home Equity Loan	$15,000	$11,500
After		
GHI Finance	Account Closed	$0
JKL Finance Home Equity Loan	Account Closed	$0

Loans with finance companies are paid down and closed.

79. Finance Companies with a Late Payment

◆━━━━━━━━━━━━━━━━━━━━━━━━━━━━━━━━━━━━━━◆

Prevent late payments from loans with high risk lenders

Another scenario that can rapidly raise the level of risk and drop our credit scores fast is having the combination of an active loan with a high risk lender and late payments. Such a combination can cause extensive damage to our credit score and makes it substantially more difficult to recover.

Those of us who have or have had a loan with a high risk lender has already increased our level of credit risk. There are questions whether we can qualify for a loan from a respected lender such as a banking institution or national credit card company. It appears we can only qualify for loans from such high risk lenders.

With any situation, a late payment is a concerning problem. Its effect on our scores can last for years. When the late payments occur with finance companies and payday lenders, the negative impact is compounded. The warning signs of *"Too many consumer finance company accounts"* (6) and *"Level of delinquency on accounts"* (2) can factor into scores for years. The greater number of late payments with high risk loans, the more severe the credit score crash. Depending on how recent the late payment occurred, credit scores can drop 100 points or more from such a situation.

If we ever have a late payment with a finance company account, the best strategy is to target this account as the first to be paid off. Any available cash flow or savings we have should be applied to pay off this account as soon as possible. Otherwise, the hole is deeper and more difficult for us to dig out. The best solution is to never be enticed by their solicitations and stay away from this danger zone.

Payment History

Credit Report Date: 1/01/2007

Creditor	**Balance**	**Payment History**
SRD Finance	$278	121111111111 (2 - 11/06)
RTS Quick Cash	$411	433211111111 (4 - 12/06) (11/06)

Two loans with a finance company and a payday lender that has late payments. "1" means current, "2" is 30 days late, "3" is 60 days late, and "4" is 90 days late.

80. New Loan with a Late Payment

Greater risk when a new loan has a late payment

Having a new loan whether it be a mortgage, auto, or credit card is always an added risk. When we establish a new loan and then we have a late payment, this recipe is one of potential disaster. This combination is a common problem and can really drop our credit scores. New loans should never have late payments.

A loan is considered new when it is opened in the last 12 months. Late payments usually happen within the first 24 months of a loan. We may be overextended or unfamiliar with payment dates. When a new loan has a late payment, the credit risk is compounded and the score can drop 100 points or more. The eventual impact from a late payment on new loans depends on the type of accounts, the balances owed, and the debt or loan balance ratio.

Two credit risk factors will primarily impact score when a new loan has a late payment. *"Too many accounts recently opened,"* (9), and *"Time since delinquency is too recent or unknown"* (13) come together to drop our scores. There is really only one or two good options.

We can minimize the level of risk by paying off the account as soon as possible. Since new loans generally have higher balances, the ability to pay them off can be difficult. Our options may be limited since our scores in most cases have dropped substantially. To refinance the loan, the interest rate on the new loan will likely be higher. We could also possibly transfer the amount owed to another outstanding line of credit.

We should become aware when new loan payments are due to make sure timely payments are made. We should also have a reserve account to help us if we encounter any financial crisis. Such a combination can keep our scores lower until the account has been paid off and the late payment eventually drops from our report.

Payment History

Credit Report Date: 1/01/2007

Creditor	Date Open	Payment History
LMN Bank	8/06	1121 (2 - 10/06)
QRS Home Equity	4/06	122111111 (2 - 11/06)

Both loans have been opened in the last eight months and also had late payments.

81. High Ratios on New Loans

Avoid borrowing entire lines against new revolving accounts

We open credit card accounts, home equity loans, and other revolving lines of credit when we finance a purchase or transfer balances from higher interest rate accounts. When we open and borrow the entire limit against a new revolving account, we can drop our scores. When we do this with multiple new accounts, we magnify our level of credit risk and we can drop our scores up to 100 points or more.

Our scores are impacted by any new account. Our scores really drop when we open multiple accounts with high debt ratios. Two credit card accounts from the same bank both have a $5,000 credit limits and $4,500 balances. One account was recently opened while the other is ten years old. Even though both accounts impact scores, the greater impact on scores will be felt from the new account.

In most cases, we open new revolving accounts when we need them. We go to *Macys*, *Sears*, or *Home Depot* to purchase an expensive item and finance the purchase. When we apply for financing, the creditor usually approves our line of credit for the amount of the purchase. Our debt ratio will be close to 100%. At the same time, we may find a lower interest rate credit card and transfer balances from higher rate accounts to this new line of credit. In many situations, we charge a substantial amount or even take out the entire line of credit on these new accounts for our immediate needs.

We can work around this issue by recognizing ways to limit the impact from new debt on our scores. If we plan ahead, we may open accounts and let them mature before we carry a balance. With the case of department store accounts, we can borrow against them to receive the discount, and then pay them off or transfer the balance to a more established account within a month or two. We may purchase a home using a second mortgage which is a common practice used by lenders to lower a monthly payment. Instead of using a credit line, we can use a fixed end (installment) second mortgage which has less impact on our scores.

Opening multiple revolving lines of credit in succession and borrowing the entire amount is the most common mistake we make with our scores. The best scenario would be to open revolving accounts and have little to no balance until they have matured at least a year. This would reduce the impact from new accounts on our scores. If we must borrow against the new accounts, we should definitely make sure the debt ratios stay below 50%.

82. High Risk Lenders & Ratios

Avoid high debt ratios with high risk lenders

Finance companies and payday lenders regularly solicit their current customers with pre-approved personal lines of credit such as home equity loans and credit cards. We should practically never have a combination of high debt ratios from a high risk lender.

Credit scores can be pummeled by the combined risk from a loan with a high risk lender and a high debt ratio. The downward spiral is more if the loan is new. *"Too many consumer finance company accounts"* (6), and *"Proportion to balance to credit limits is too high on revolving accounts"* (10) usually appear as the highest impacting factors on a score. If the loan is new, *"Too many accounts recently opened"* (9) is a third risk factor that can also affect scores. Any such combination can see credit scores drop up to 100 points or more. It is a poisonous combination for credit scores. The result can be quick and can take years of our excruciating hard work for a score to recover to respectable levels.

This combination comes from home equity loans or other personal lines of credit from finance companies. This is the scenario that dropped Brian's credit score in the introduction of this publication. When we realize that our credit scores have declined, we may have no real option but to pay down the loan with our own funds. Since our scores could substantially drop, the interest rate on a new loan from a quality lender would be substantially higher — that is even if we could qualify.

A *"Big danger"* warning sign should be displayed to everyone considering a new loan with this type of lender and loan. We should never take out a loan with a high debt ratio on a revolving loan from a high risk lender. Regardless of any present concern, we should look elsewhere for our financing to protect our score.

Payment History

Credit Report Date: 1/01/2007

Creditor	Opening Date	Credit Limit	Balance
Before			
IHG Finance	11/06	$1,500	$1,500
After			
IHG Finance	11/06	Account Closed	$0

Loan with finance company is paid off and closed.

13

Identity Theft

Rick had worked overseas in a foreign country for a couple of years. Upon his return to the United States, he had a quick surprise. Not only was his identity stolen, it was taken by a person very close to him in his family, his father. The damage was extensive and dropped his credit score over two hundred points as payments went late from multiple opened loans.

He had few options. The creditors would release him from the liability of the loans under one option: a police report had to be filed. With a police report, a subsequent investigation would be completed and a possible prosecution of the crime against his father. A tough decision considering the person who used his identity was the last person he ever thought would commit such an offense against him.

Rick elected to forego the police report and filed a Chapter 7 bankruptcy. His credit was ruined. He would have to start picking up the pieces and always worry about his father stealing his identity once his credit score was re-established. The one advantage Rick has over many victims of identity theft, he knew the perpetrator.

Everyone is talking about identity theft primarily since there has been several large breaches of security at some large companies. Everyone is at risk. Identity theft is growing like a rolling thunderstorm. With the addition of the internet, that thunderstorm is growing at enormous rates and the only question is, *"Who will be caught out in the storm and who will be safe inside?"*

A 2003 U.S. Federal Trade Commission reports that almost one in ten Americans have been victims to identity theft in the preceding five years. The average loss for each case of identity theft was $10,200 for financial institutions and $2,100 for victims. There is usually no greater desperate financial feeling than to have our identity stolen. The time and cost to repair the damage can be enormous.

In a combined study from the Javelin Strategy and Research and the Better Business Bureau released in January 2007, this study reports that 63% of the identity theft cases were the result from someone close to us such as family, friends, or neighbors stealing our identity; or were the result of a lost or stolen wallet, checkbook, credit card, mail, or breach in a home computer system. This study and Rick's personal story highlights the necessity for us to not only work with companies that have systems in place, but also to protect our identity at home. Once our personal identity is compromised, the effort to recover our information can be never ending. Once the fire starts, where it goes, no one can tell.

We should all recognize areas that are more vulnerable to theft. We should be extremely careful in who we give our personal information. Credit scores can be greatly affected by the crime of identity theft. We need to be better policemen of our personal information. Protecting personal information is extremely critical in maintaining a high credit score. We should protect our social security number, birth date, and other personal information. The higher the credit score, the more valuable and attractive that our identity is to thieves. We should take steps now to protect our identity.

No one can take measures that can prevent identification theft with a 100% surety. Nevertheless, we all need to ask questions and take preventative actions now rather than think that identity theft will never happen to us. A few measures of caution can go a long way in the protection of our personal information.

This chapter outlines strategies to protect identification from being stolen, use of measures to protect our assets and identify areas to protect credit scores. If our identity is stolen, this chapter also outlines the steps to take to protect our identity, our credit information, and our credit scores.

83. Social Security Number

Limit access to a few quality companies

The social security number is the foundation of our credit files, and ultimately, our credit scores. If someone has access to all nine digits of our social security number, that person can practically create a new identification with a new name. Some measures have been taken by the major credit bureaus to protect us from having someone establish a new identification. Nevertheless, we should limit its availability.

The more access people have to our social security number, the greater probability that our identity can be stolen. When we submit credit applications to multiple lenders in person, by telephone, or online, we expose ourselves to identity theft. Limiting our social security number's availability can reduce the number of companies and people with access to our personal information.

When looking for a mortgage, auto or other lender, we should identify a direct lender who usually does not sell their loans to outside lenders. Our information can then be kept with one company. An auto or mortgage broker creates more opportunities for having an identity stolen by sending our personal information to multiple lenders. When utilizing a broker's services, we are usually unaware of the individuals or companies that are looking at our personal information. When we utilize a direct lender, less individuals are involved minimizing the opportunities for identity theft.

We should also use a lender that does not sell our personal information to outside companies. Companies oftentimes sell personal information to outside lenders and marketing firms for additional revenue. If there is a question, we should ask the company if they sell our personal information to outside companies. Many lenders today should provide a written disclosure notifying us of the companies' intentions to sell our personal information.

We should all ask, identify, and use lenders and other financial services companies that do not sell personal information. By using those companies that lend their own money and by limiting the visibility of a social security number and other personal information, we can take major steps to protect our identity. These are steps are small, but very important in protecting our credit score.

84. Review All Inquiries

Identify companies looking at our credit report

Each major credit bureau compiles an *Inquiries* section with each credit file. This list identifies those companies that have requested our credit report over the last 24 months. When reviewing this section, we may fail to recognize some of the companies requesting our credit report. In some cases, we never granted permission. Reviewing the inquiries listed in our credit report helps us identify those companies looking at our credit report, and discover any possible irregularities.

When companies request our credit report, they have access to our most intimate personal information. Companies request credit information for lending, insurance, employment, collection, and marketing purposes. Since there can be marketing requests for future promotions, we sometimes may not recognize all those companies that have requested our credit report. To help us understand inquiries, some credit reports separate the different uses for our credit report into lending, promotional, and account reviews, in the *Inquiries* section.

We should identify all parties requesting our report by reviewing the *Inquiries* section of our credit report. A list of companies, the report dates, and the credit bureau are displayed for two years. The first sign of identity theft is usually with an unrecognizable inquiry.

When someone has accessed our credit report, we need to identify the purpose of their request. If a particular inquiry is not from a recognized lender or for lending purposes, we need to get additional information. The credit report usually has a business number to the company that requested our credit report. We should call and ask the company the purpose and any required authorization to make sure our identity has not been stolen.

By reviewing the *Inquiries* section of the credit report, we can better manage our personal information, limit the availability of our personal information, and take measures to prevent identity theft and our scores.

Inquiries

Companies	Date	Credit Bureau
EFG Financial	01/04/2006	EFX
JIH Bank	01/07/2006	TU
RST Marketing	01/21/2006	XPN
WXY Employment Services	01/30/2006	EFX

85. Personal Record Keeping

A safe to maintain and a shredder to destroy documents

A quick look around the house and we can usually find a lot of personal information hanging around. There are tax statements with social security numbers, credit card account numbers, and checking and savings account numbers. We must identify what personal information to keep and what information to throw away. Since identity at home occurs at higher levels, we must create a system to safety keep and to properly destroy the personal documentation.

To protect from identity theft, we should create a system to protect our personal information. Personal tax returns, W2's, checking and savings account statements should be retained for several years to document personal tax information. Other information such as pay stubs and credit card offers should generally not be held for long. All personal information should eventually be discarded. A personal system should be set up to identify when and where to keep, and how often to discard, our personal information.

To protect those items that are retained in a home, we should invest in something secure where personal information can be kept for possible future references. A filing cabinet or safe with a lock can be suited to store our personal information. Any personal information that must be retained should be kept in that secure location. As months and years pass by, we should recognize how long any particular information must be retained. When the time has passed, the information should be securely discarded.

For information that needs to be discarded, we should invest in a shredder. Any personal information that is not needed, promotional offers, or information that is generally five years or older should be discarded with a shredder. Many thieves have rummaged through people's residential garbage finding personal information. They have even taken discarded pre-approved credit card offers to steal an identity.

By creating a viable system and taking measures of prevention, we take prudent steps to protect ourselves from identity theft. The better organized we are in managing our personal information, the more control we have. By both creating a workable disposal system and having a secured cabinet for personal items, we can take strong measures against identity theft.

86. Company's Disposal Methods

Verify discarding methods before applying

When we apply for a loan, insurance, or other services, we usually provide personal information to validate our income, asset, debt, and credit information to various companies. Most times, we are unaware the final destiny of our personal information. We should be better aware of the methods used by these firms before we pass along our personal information. Many companies have inadequate means to dispose of confidential information and no government oversight to properly handle personal information.

Many larger companies have now instituted guidelines to dispose of personal information no longer needed. Many smaller companies, however, lack the financial resources or fail to recognize the threat and do not have adequate systems that is required to protect personal information. When reviewing terms on a loan or other financial services, we should ask what methods the company has established to maintain and to dispose of our personal information. The critical documentation that should be protected by companies include social security numbers, birthdays, account numbers, and addresses. Even a slightly better interest rate cannot offset the risk associated from having an identity stolen. The risk is too great!

We should never be afraid or embarrassed to ask someone what methods they have established to discard of our personal information. Many identities have been stolen when companies have failed to properly dispose personal documentation. If we recognize that a company has no set policies, we should look for a different company who has such policies. We can even contact any third party security or paper shredding firm to verify that they service a particular company.

Many companies today have contracted with firms that go to their offices and shred personal documentation on-site. Other areas of protection include encryption on their computer systems, and limiting access to people's personal information from even those working for the company. Encryption makes it extremely difficult for someone outside the company to pull personal information from computer systems.

Even though there is no perfect system of protecting our personal information, each additional policy helps to protect personal documentation and information. Companies that have policies and systems in place should be utilized. The cost of one mishap is too great and could cost a person thousands of dollars, let alone an excellent credit score.

87. Mail Box

Have a secured mail box that limits access

What is the easiest method for someone to steal our personal identity? How often is our social security number, bank account numbers, birth-dates, and other personal information received through the mail? What if a thief had access to all the information that came in our mail? Would our personal information be compromised? What personal in-formation can someone take by taking our mail?

Criminals target mail as one of the easiest methods to steal personal information. Anyone who has access to our mail could probably gather documentation on company names, credit card and account numbers, and even social security numbers. Mail theft is up in almost every major city across the country because of the available information found in our mail.

In order to guard against identification theft, we should all have a mail box with a lock. Protecting the mail with a locked mail box is a simple, but valuable measure. Even when we are out of town, a locked mail box may prevent someone from taking our mail. By taking this important measure, we have some security prevention against mail thieves. A small cost today is the insurance policy we take out against a bigger problem tomorrow.

We should not only be concerned with incoming mail, but also outgo-ing mail. Many of the letters we mail out also have personal informa-tion in them. We should never mail letters with personal information from our residential mail box unless its access is limited to the mail-man. Tax returns, checks, credit card or banking account statements should be sent from a post office. By taking a few extra minutes, we can limit access to this mail to just the employees at the post office.

Many identity theft victims have found that their identity was stolen from their mail box. In one reported instance, a postal customer was caught trying to lift the mail from the deposit slot at the post office. What was the purpose? The person was looking for checks inside of envelopes with corresponding routing and account numbers. Once the information is taken, money can be accessed.

A simple, but effective method, can be a barrier from those who want our identity. By having a locked mail box and mailing our bills directly from the post office, we can protect ourselves from mail thieves.

88. Personal Check Dangers

Limit use of personal checks

A common method for some criminals is to access the personal information taken from our personal checks. When checks are the primary method used to make payment for gas, groceries, or other daily purchases, we allow others access to our personal information written on our checks. Addresses and account numbers can easily be lifted and be used to steal our identity and our good credit.

Checking accounts are the financial lifeline for many of us. Our checks access our personal accounts and contain vital information. This simplicity of the system is also the disadvantage. Information written on our personal check includes our name and address, the banking institution, the bank routing and account numbers, and sometimes our social security number. Similar to debit cards, we are giving private information to the public eye when paying by personal check.

When a personal check's information is exploited for improper use, money can be taken directly from our accounts. Retail clerks, managers, and other individuals can easily pull our information and create a new identity. They then could have access to our cash assets and possibly credit. If we commonly used personal checks, there is no real protection against a criminal taking the information displayed on them.

The damage created for any person can be extremely untimely. Money can be taken so that overdraft accounts are used, accounts are closed and other checks are returned. Credit lines can be overrun and retail outlets can send returned checks to collection. All of which can affect a our credit file and score. The time, effort, and cost to recover our identity and the damage created can be extensive.

We should limit the use of personal checks to necessary purchases. Our checks should only be used for bills that are paid to a person or company we are familiar, or through the mail. We should not use them with every purchase for gas, groceries, or other daily expenses. Rather, we should use means to limit their access to the public eye. We can use other less intrusive means of payment such as credit cards. By limiting the visibility of our checking account, we can limit the access to some very personal information. We can protect our identity and our valued credit scores.

89. Debit Cards

Limit use of debit cards for everyday purchases

Debit card have fast become the choice of payment over the last few years. Even with its pin number that is meant to protect access to the account, debit cards can still pose a real threat to a our money and credit rating. Anyone who can break through or who has unauthorized access to the personal identification number (PIN) can have unlimited access to a our account with its money and available lines of credit. Theft of debit card information can potentially affect our credit rating.

Debit cards have been used as a means to replace cash payments for purchases. We can avoid carrying cash and the concerns of being robbed. The debit card replaces cash as a reliable form of payment. Identity thieves are not interested in someone's personal information. Rather, they are more interested in the money. Identity theft is only used as a means to an end. If thieves could access a our checking account directly, they would bypass taking someone's identity.

More reports have recently surfaced of criminals accessing money from someone's debit card. With debit cards, thieves can steal money directly out of an account within minutes by simply accessing the information on the debit card. Each debit card transaction should carry a *Personal Identification Number* (PIN) that should only be decoded by the bank. PINs, however, can be stolen in a variety of ways that are too difficult to prevent. Because of this danger, we should understand the dangers and even limit the use of debit cards.

In the case of a fraudulent purchases with a debit card, we may have to work with the bank to recover the stolen money. In addition, the overdraft account may have been compromised which can have a direct impact on our credit rating. We can protect ourselves by using a credit card. Credit cards in most cases have greater protections against theft and fraudulent transactions than debit cards. We can simply cancel a transaction and then the burden of proof goes to the company that charged our credit card. If the purchase is not from the person on the credit card, the liability can eventually be taken from the consumer.

We can charge our monthly expenses to our credit card and then payoff the account every month. By using a credit card instead of a debit card, we create another barrier against would-be thieves. Personal assets can then be guarded, liability greatly reduced, and a credit score protected.

90. Pre-Approved Credit Card Offers

We can opt out of many of the free credit card offers

Most every one of us has received pre-approved credit card offers in the mail. These offers often come from companies that we have never heard of. We usually have never had an open account with them let alone given our personal information to them. *How do they generate these pre-approved offers?*

These offers are usually generated from credit bureau lists. A common marketing practice for many credit card and mortgage lenders is to purchase lists of qualified borrowers from sources such as the credit bureaus. Companies pay the credit bureaus for these lists. The creditors then send credit card offers to those of us who are qualified.

As these offers are being given, personal information is being circulated. Our information is being bought and sold as a commodity between companies. As our personal information becomes more available, our identity is vulnerable to theft. Our identity can also be stolen by someone intercepting one of the pre-approved offers.

How can we take greater control of the sale of our information? We can request that our personal information not be sold. If we are concerned, we should be pro-active and request that our personal information not be sold. Any person who wants to limit most of the free credit card offers can call the following number and request their name be removed from marketing lists that are sold to lenders:

1-888-5opt-out

The credit bureaus are then required to remove our name from future marketing lists. This limits the access by secondary companies to our personal information. Pre-approved offers should slow down as a our information is no longer openly available to market.

However, creditors can still gain some access to our information. Current or past lenders may still sell our information to outside companies to generate revenue. If we want to limit these pre-approved offers, it is important that we use companies that do not sell our information. Calling the above number and requesting our name be removed from marketing lists and carefully selecting lenders adds protection to our personal information.

91. Family Identity Theft

Review our family member's credit reports for misuse

One of the biggest increase in identification theft is the misuse of our children's and older American's personal information. Parents and guardians alike should not only be concerned with their own personal information, but also the personal information of their dependents. Their social security numbers and other personal information can be accessed and new identities created without much detection.

Trying to locate a valid social security number is not a difficult proposition. The first three digits of a social security number are usually determined by the state where the person resided the moment the social security number was given. Figuring out the remaining digits is less difficult. When children or aging adults have their identity stolen, the time to discover the crime is usually much longer.

There are several potential signs of such identity theft. A pre-approved credit offer may come in a child's name. A grandparent may receive unrecognizable collection calls. In some cases because they don't have any debt, they usually brush this aside offer or ignore a collection call as a wrong number or mistake. A creditor may eventually file a claim in court against the wrong person. Every possible sign should be investigated to protect against fraud.

One of the more egregious crimes is when a parent steals the identity of their own children. They use the child's personal information to attain financing. Recent cases of identity theft have included parents or relatives of the children. How parents can use the identity of a child or aging adult is beyond any comprehension. When the child arrives at 18 years old, his credit may be awash in debt and collections.

Every guardian needs to be pro-active to protect their family's personal information. Credit reports should be requested from the credit bureaus on a periodic basis in children's and parent's names. Review all the information and make sure that all creditors are recognized in the report. We should contact the lender when we fail to recognize a loan or a lender. By requesting credit bureau reports and recognizing unexpected offers in the mail, we can track our dependent's credit information. This can shorten the time after a problem occurs to realize the signs of identity theft.

92. Credit Monitoring Services

Understand their services and their limitations

Growth in credit monitoring services has been phenomenal. These services are offered by many companies as a viable method to quickly identify misuse of our credit. Every one of us who signs up for these services should understand their limitations. They are not always a catch-all for identity theft.

The fact that credit agencies are profiting from monitoring services is ironic since they are a major part of the identity theft problem. If they had a better and more efficient system, we would not have to purchase credit monitoring services to protect our personal information.

Credit monitoring services are sold as a means to track a person's credit file. Such companies as *Identify Guard, Citi, TrueCredit, Experian, Equifax*, and others offer services to monitor credit. Since they offer varying levels of services, we should understand what they agree to do and their limitations. The credit monitoring services may or may not catch an instance of identity theft.

We should first identify what credit bureaus or credit files they monitor. Many services do not watch all three credit files. If someone steals our identity, we may not know it since the monitoring service was watching *Experian* when the identification was taken from *Equifax*.

Second, some companies offer alert reports that can be spaced as much as three months. Our identity could have been taken up to three months before it is caught. A lot of damage can happen in that amount of time. Other companies offer alerts every few weeks. The shorter period with the greater number of credit bureaus monitored, the more costly the service. Some of the services even offer an insurance policy which may be helpful to counter losses.

There can be many gaps in the creditor monitoring services. If we want to utilize these services, we should review each offer by going through their information on their web sites and utilizing consumer reports. Having an identity already stolen or being concerned with possible theft, such individuals should probably select a service to monitor their credit with the greatest protection for the foreseeable future.

Understanding what each company offers and its limitations can identify areas of needed protection for our credit file and score.

93. Stolen Identity!

◆━━━◆

Identify what to do, our rights and protections

When the frightening discovery occurs that our personal identification has been stolen, we should take immediate steps to prevent its damage. The faster we act to protect our identity usually results in less problems and less cost for us in the future.

Once we notice that our identification has been compromised, we should immediately contact the following institutions:

1. Creditors that are involved
2. Banking institutions with checking accounts and debit cards
3. Credit bureaus to get a fraud alert
4. FTC ID theft hotline
5. Police to file a report

Depending on what has been compromised, we should contact lenders, banking institutions, the theft hotline, and credit card companies immediately. Every company that has our assets or our credit information should be notified of the crime.

After creditors and banks have been contacted, we should contact the Federal Trade Commission I.D. theft hotline at 1-877-438-4338. Additional calls should be made to at least one of the credit bureaus to notify them of the identity theft: Credit bureaus are subsequently required to notify each other in the event of one notification of identity theft.

Equifax	1-800-525-6285
Experian	1-888-397-3742
Trans Union	1-800-680-7289

When a fraud alert has been given, new loans cannot be opened until the creditor calls to verify the person really applying for credit and two, picture identifications from government sources are provided.

Finally, a police report should be filed. Some creditors require that a police report be filed before any action can be taken against fraudulent charges. The faster we act, the greater chance of preventing credit and financial misuse. Once our identity has been compromised, we may have to go through a lot to take out a loan and we may have to use credit monitoring services for an extended period of time.

94. Personal Information

Keep personal information from public eyes

Practically everyone has at least one computer and one cell phone. We sometimes communicate personal information through these channels of communication. We should however should use caution when passing our personal information through a computer and a cell phone.

Such information as social security numbers, birthdates, mother's maiden name, address, account, and credit card numbers should always be kept private. The concern is granting unauthorized access to unknown people who use these channels of communication.

We talk and receive communication though wireless phones. These phones are not secured lines of communication. Anyone with some technical sophistication can intercept our phone calls. Personal information can be compromised and an identity stolen through such communications. Thieves are persistent and can find many areas to track our personal information.

Another concern is the use of online computers and wireless computers. Technical experts confirm that any firewall and password can be compromised. Since most of us have a considerable amount of personal information on our computer, a criminal could access this information with a little time. A computer and its online connection should be turned off to protect our personal information.

Personal information should not under any circumstance be transferred using wireless technology. Even though there are safeguards, wireless communication passes through public airwaves. A person using a remote for their computer can possibly tap into our wireless connection.

One slip up and our personal information can become public. Be smart and limit personal information from being publicly broadcast. Internet connections should be shut down so that no one can pull information from our computer. Common sense can help us protect our identity.

14

The Road to 850

Where do we start? Where do we go? How do we make the best decisions now so that our credit scores increase faster? The challenge of the credit scoring system is recognizing where we are and where we want to go. There is no one clear immediate answer for everyone. What could be the best strategy for one could be detrimental for another. For this reason, the credit scoring system is not easy to comprehend. It has many winding roads and terms that are difficult to understand. Understanding the system and the road signs helps us develop greater insight so that we can implement a plan that helps us arrive at our destination.

Except for those who are establishing a new credit file, we all have some credit and are at some point down the *Road to 850*. Even though two individuals may have the same score, they have arrived at that score using different means. This indicates that similar people with the same scores can be going in separate directions facing diverse issues. Each must apply different strategies to increase their scores.

There are three questions we need to address when we set out strategies with our credit scores.

> 1. What is my credit score?
> 2. What do I want my credit score to be?
> 3. How do I increase my current score?

The first two questions are fairly easy. The third question requires planning and action to increase our credit scores. We can wish to have a certain credit score, but if we don't plan and work through a n effective plan, we may never arrive at our desired score.

1. *What is my credit score?*

When was the last time we were told our credit score? Do we remember that three digit number and do we know what factors were hurting our score? If we have not been given our credit score by either a lender or pulling it directly in the last ninety days, we should find out. We can either go back to a recent lender and ask, or pull our credit score online. The best recommendation is to go online at www.myfico.com for accurate credit score.

2. *What do I want my credit score to be?*

Many of us will give different answers because we may be unfamiliar with the ramifications of a credit score. We may be fine with a 700 or even a 650 score. However, such scores can cost us extra money from higher insurance premiums and interest rates. Ultimately, we should work to have an excellent credit score that is between 760 and 850. Most preferably, we should work to have a credit score in the 800s.

3. *How do I increase my credit score and what is my time frame?*

Brett and Erin have two things in common and they don't even know each other. They both have a 668 FICO (Experian) credit score and want to purchase their first home. Brett has worked at a local tire center for four years. He has been married for five years and has one young child.

Erin is 20 years old, recently married, and moved into a two bedroom apartment. She has been working at a local restaurant for one year as a shift manager. As we look through their individual credit reports, their profiles are equally different.

Brett has four accounts with balances. He has a $14,600 auto loan open for six months at his local credit union. He also has an $425 personal loan taken out two months prior at the credit union. His last two loans are from department stores; Sears and Wal-Mart. Sears has been open for eight and a half years while the Wal-Mart account was just recently opened. They both have small balances around $500.

Brett had a late payment on an auto loan 18 months ago. He also had three judgments five years ago that have since been paid. Last of all, he has one collection account two years old and a Discover account that fell three months behind in payments six years ago.

Erin on the other hand has only had three total credit references in her file. She had a credit card that was open for only two years and closed

---

Brett   Credit Score: 668

Reason Codes:
1.   (38) Serious delinquency and derogatory public record or collection filed.
2.   (18) Number of accounts delinquent.
3.   (10) Proportion of balances to high credit on revolving accounts.
4.   (14) Length of time accounts have been established.

Erin   Credit Score: 668

Reason Codes:
1.   (14) Length of time accounts have been established.
2.   (10) Proportion of balances to high credit on revolving accounts.
3.   (1) Amount owed on accounts is too high.
4.   (8) Number of recent inquiries.

---

it four months ago. She has two open accounts, one a bank auto loan for $11,400, and a bank credit card account with a balance of $2,000 that were both opened in the last eight months.

Even though Brett and Erin have the same credit scores, their reason codes reflect different issues. Brett has had late payments, a collection, and judgments in his credit history and they are all hurting his score. This will take several more years before these issues disappear from his credit report. He must address other concerns in the short term to raise his score. Even though his accounts with Sears ($563) and Wal-Mart ($537) are small balances, they are impacting his score. The credit limit on Sears is $1,000 and Wal-Mart is $975. He should pay down both balances below 50%, or raise the credit limits above $1,200. Finally, he needs to keep his current accounts open so that he can develop some depth in his credit file.

Erin has a very limited credit file. She needs to develop a stronger credit file by leaving her current accounts open for as long as possible to build depth. She should open an additional revolving account, bank or merchant account some time in the next year. She doesn't need to borrow against them, only establish additional account references. The best time to open revolving accounts is when we don't need to borrow against them. If she opens accounts in the next year, she can spread out her new loans so that they do not affect her score as much in the short term. Last of all, she should pay down the balance on her bank credit account because she has a $2,000 balance with a $3,5000 credit limit. She should reduce that balance down to at least $1750.

Practically no two people have the same plan. Each situation, plan, and strategy is different. The challenge of the credit system is identifying the best steps for each of us to take to arrive at our desired location without wasting our time, effort, and money. When we make the best decisions now, we can see a higher credit score in the coming months.

It is like driving from Los Angeles to New York City. We wouldn't drive through Seattle and then to Atlanta before we went to New York City. If our primary destination is New York City, we would want to drive straight from Los Angeles. We may use different roads and arrive at different times. It is the same philosophy with the credit scoring system. We want the correct answers now so that we can arrive within our time schedule.

That time schedule is usually determined by some pressing need. *When do I need my credit score at that level in the future? Are we looking to purchase a home, a car, or are we changing employment?* These questions will help us determine our strategies. We usually ask these questions when we face a problem and it too late in many instances.

When we are addressing, *"What do I need to do and what is my time frame?"*, there are three primary steps that will help us arrive at the desired credit score — 760 to 850. These three keys are:

1. **Become Educated.**
2. **Identify Areas of Concern.**
3. **Create Short and Long Term Strategies.**

We have learned that having too little or too many of one particular account can hurt our score. We can have none or too much loan activity that can drop our scores. *What is the correct level of credit so that we can increase our scores?* Understanding acceptable levels of credit, identifying areas of concern, and implementing a compatible short and long term plan that meets our time table are all important to reach our desired goal.

Become Educated

Where can we go if we don't know where we are going or are going in the wrong direction? The first signs of our direction are the reasons codes that come with our credit scores. These codes provide personal directions for each of us to identify areas of concern. If we have an established credit file and we just recently opened accounts, pay off and close some of them. If we have high balances on our revolving accounts, we can pay them down. If we need more length of time with our accounts, we should keep all our current accounts open indefinitely especially those opened the longest.

The Reason Codes reveal the items we should have, and those issues we should avoid in our credit file. Here is a list:

What we should have:
1. At least one active revolving (preferably a bank or national credit card) account that is regularly used. *(Page 46 / Codes 15, 16, 24, & 29)*
2. At least one installment loan. *(Page 13 / Code 32 or 4)*
3. Mature accounts. *(Page 77 / Codes 12 & 14)*

What we should avoid:
1. Any late payments. *(Page 74 / Codes 2, 13, 21, & 39)*
2. Any public records or collections. *(Pages 127 –130 / Codes 2, 38, & 40)*
3. Any excessively high balances on credit cards or other unsecured lines of credit. *(Page 53 / Code 11)*
4. High debt and loan balance ratios. *(Pages 54 & 65 / Codes 10 & 33 or 3)*
5. Finance companies. *(Page 48 / Code 6)*
6. Excessive number of open accounts. *(Page 80 / Code 28)*
7. Excessive number of accounts with balances. *Page 81 / Code 5)*
8. Excessive number of open revolving accounts with banks or national credit card companies (Both with and without balances). *(Page 60 / Codes 4 & 23)*
9. New accounts. *(Page 76 / Code 9)*
10. Inquiries. *(Page 30 / Code 8)*

We need at least one open bank or national revolving account with some recent activity, one open installment loan, an unspotted payment history, a limited number of accounts with balances, some time between opening new accounts, and finally low debt and loan balance ratios.

We don't necessarily need to take on debt to build a credit score. We can use a credit card from a bank or national credit card company for our purchases instead of a debit card and then pay off the account at the end of each month. We can work the system and build a score no matter what our financial situation.

Identify Areas of Concern

This can be a tougher step if we are unfamiliar of the credit score requirements. Nevertheless, it is a very important step. Once we recognize those reason codes and their negative impact on our credit score, we need to translate those issues in our credit report. We need to know what our reason codes are trying to tell us in our credit report. We need to identify those issues that are affecting our score.

Larry had work extremely hard over the last three years to pay for all his bills. He had paid them with cash because he did not want to take

Larry's credit score showed as follows:

Larry   Credit Score: 629

Reason Codes:
1. (40) Derogatory public record or collection filed.
2. (20) Length of time since derogatory public record or collection is too short.
3. (30) Time since recent account opening is too short.
4. (10) Proportion of balances to high credit on revolving accounts.

on any new debt. Larry wanted to buy a house, but was extremely distraught because he had no credit score. He had applied for a personal loan at his bank and was denied. The bank's loan officer told him it would take five years for him to get one. He thought that there was no hope to buy a house because he could not be approved for a mortgage.

As he reviewed his credit, he had several concerns. Larry's wife had many medical bills that went to a collection agency. The collections were old and there was no loan activity in the last 12 months. Hence, no credit score (or reason code) was provided by the credit bureaus.

He reviewed his report with an experienced mortgage lender and identify several concerns. He had no recent loan activity and the only credit references in his credit report were collections. He had to pay off his collections and establish some new quality credit references. Larry could reestablish credit scores once some new accounts were opened.

He took out a couple of secured bank revolving accounts to establish some new account references. Within a few months, a 629 credit score appeared and Larry was subsequently approved for an auto loan, financed through an auto manufacturer. Three months later, he bought his first home.

As with Brett, Erin, and Larry, we each have different issues. Most of us are somewhere along the *Road to 850*. Knowing what to do is the second step after we have identified what issues are keeping our score from progressing higher and arriving at our desired destination. Our effectiveness in translating the information found in the reason codes will determine how fast we can go. If we can properly read the road signs, we can know the best direction to go.

Short and Long Term Strategies *(The Element of Time)*

With Larry, he created several strategies - short and long term strategies. His short term strategy included re-establishing some quality credit references. His long term strategies are more challenging and take time: establish a clean payment record and create depth in his credit file. He left those two credit cards open to let them establish some depth in his file. His credit score increased to over 700 within a year. An 800 score could be reached in a few years down the road as long as he stays within his plan.

Some strategies can be completed within 30 to 90 days. Short term strategies can raise our credit scores within a few months. Other strategies take longer. We want a report clear of any derogatory credit and have multiple *golden accounts*. These two strategies can take time. It is best that we identify those strategies now so that we don't get down the road and find out we are where we were two years ago. Long term strategies are extremely important because it is from them that we can reach an excellent credit score in the 800s

Michael had worked at a national shipping firm for several years. He was in the midst of a Chapter 13 bankruptcy that would be completed in another 18 months. Even though his credit score was 527, his credit was dismal. There was only a couple of quality references and they were several years old. Every account with a balance was in the bankruptcy and he had to wait until the bankruptcy discharged to establish any new credit.

He developed a plan with a credit specialist. He had to wait for the court to discharge the bankruptcy before he could establish new credit. As soon as the bankruptcy discharged in May 2005, he opened a couple of new accounts. One was a secured credit card with a bank and the second was an offer that came through the mail. Over the next year, he continued to correct his credit file from the bankruptcy when they failed to update a $0 loan balance. After 30 months of work; and within twelve months of the discharge, Michael's credit score had risen to 652, an increase of 125 points!

Chuck, on the other hand, had a 525 credit score. He had co-signed on his sister's loan which subsequently fell past due several payments. He contacted the lender about this poor rating. Since he was a cosigner and had no knowledge of the late payments, the lender agreed to remove the late payments from his report if he brought the account current. He paid the past due amount and his score jumped to 716.

These two examples provide two success stories from various extremes. Increasing credit scores can be at times challenging and sometimes overwhelming. If we become better educated, and recognize those areas of concern, we can create more effective short and long term plans and reach our desired goal in due time.

As we drive our credit scores to 850, we should recognize those major factors that affect them. Even though the factors can vary slightly in weight with each credit score system, they are all very important. We can refer to these factors as **G.O.L.D.** *If there is anytime to go for the GOLD, it is now:*

G.	**G**ood mix of Accounts
O.	**O**n-Time Payments
L.	**L**ength of Open Accounts
D.	**D**ebt Reduction

(The credit bureaus add new accounts as a fifth factor. If we open multiple accounts, they shorten the average age of our active accounts. For this purpose, we have included it into the length of open accounts.)

Good Mix of Accounts: The proper mix of installment and revolving accounts is important to raise our credit score. We must have some activity from each type of loan, but not too much. If we lack a proper mix of accounts, we can develop a proper level within a few months.

On-Time Payments: We must develop a payment history that is free from any blemish. If we have late payments, they can drop our scores for several years. We must then develop a clean record going forward so that over time, those late payments can drop from our credit report. A clean record can take several years to develop.

Length of Accounts: The longer we have our accounts open, the better it reflects on our score. This means we must curtail the number of new loans and establish multiple mature accounts. This factor can take several years to develop if we have no depth in our active account history.

Debt Reduction: We should reduce the number of total loans with balances. We should also pay down the balances on our accounts. If we have the financial resources, we can pay down our debt and our scores will increase within a month or two. It all depends on our financial resources to pay down our debt.

As we define our strategies, they should be based on when we need our credit scores and how high they should be. We may want to buy a home or an auto. We would be wise to look a some short term strategies to raise our scores. We could pay down debt, pay off a finance company, or open an account with a bank or national credit card company.

If we don't have any pressing needs, we can look to address some of our long term concerns. We can keep our oldest accounts open indefinitely to build depth and make on-time payments to build a stronger payment history. Our short and long term strategies should be dependent on any pressing needs and our time frame.

We should develop a realistic plan that can increase our scores over time. In most instances, there are no quick fix programs available to raise a credit score 100 to 150 points within 30 days. Strategies take time to fulfill. Once the plan has been created and the strategies are implemented, we should periodically check our scores for improvement. We might request our credit score once every three to six months to update our position.

If we have personal questions, we can sit down with a qualified professional who specializes in credit scores. Such specialist should understand all the codes and factors that impact credit scores. This professional can provide directions to help us raise a credit score from 530 to 650, 650 to 750, and ultimately 750 to 800.

Once at an 800 level credit score, we can practically determine our own financial destiny. We have the power to negotiate an interest rate or premium. We won't need someone telling us what our rate or payment will be. We can negotiate lower interest rates and terms on practically every loan we take out. The challenge then is maintaining our score within our desired goal — 760 to 850. At times, we may have some financial obligations to meet and our scores may drop. Nevertheless, we can create strategies now to develop greater depth and minimize the impact on our scores later.

In whatever situation we face, we should never give up! We may already be close to arriving and simply need to shore up some issues to maintain our scores. By understanding the system, identifying our concerns, and creating short and long term strategies, we can increase our scores more rapidly. We can save ourselves literally thousands of dollars a year in extra financial charges, lower insurance premiums, or even secure better employment.

The car is running and the *Road to 850* may not be far away. We just need to determine the direction to go and start moving. Whatever it takes, it is definitely worth the time and effort to get on the road.

So, let's go!

Author's Notes

At the time of this publication, the three major credit bureaus are reviewing proposed changes to the credit scoring models. These proposed changes include having the same credit scoring model called *Vantage* for each credit score. This proposal includes following a scoring model that is easier to understand.

This proposed change would have one standard system for all the credit scores. The second change is the way that credit scores are calculated. The proposed model would have credit scores from 900-990 (A) for top levels of credit, 800-899 (B) for those with above average credit, 700-799 (C) for those with average credit, 600-699 (D) for those with fair credit, and 500-599 (F) with poor credit.

We can find those scores at each credit bureau's website. However, most lenders have not yet endorsed the *Vantage* credit score model.

Appendix
A

Credit Score Codes

Classic Model

The *Classic* credit score model is used by many lenders including mortgage lenders. We provide the outline of the various reason codes used with this model with a brief explanation.

Classic
Model

1 The utilization of loan debt in relation to the beginning loan amounts (installment accounts) and the high credit limits (revolving accounts) on all open and active accounts is high.

Equifax *Amount owed on accounts is too high.*
Experian *Current balances on accounts.*
Trans Union *Amount owed on accounts is too high.*

Explanation This issue impacts credit scores when the current debt in the credit file is being utilized at excessively high levels. This concern usually arises when we have high balances on consumer loans such as credit card, personal and auto loans. This factor often appears along side, *"Balances to high credit limits too high on revolving accounts."* (10) There are high balances in relation to the total beginning loan balances or high credit limits from all open accounts in the credit report. As we pay down our installment loan balances and we reduce the balances on open lines of credit, we can reduce this risk and its impact on credit scores. When we carry high balances, it can have a considerable effect on scores.

Strategies Refer to #28, 29, 35, & 76.

2 At least one loan has had a late payment in the credit report. We have raised our level of credit risk questioning whether we can make timely payments on the current outstanding debt. number of late payments whether

Equifax *Level of delinquency on accounts.*
Experian *Delinquency reported on accounts.*
Trans Union *Level of delinquency on accounts.*

Explanation This risk factor usually appears when there is the first late payment. It is considered a Level I delinquency. Any loan that has a late payment in its payment history affects credit scores. The question is, *"How much?"* With this issue, there is may be a late payment with one loan, or a few spread throughout the credit file. The total impact on scores is determined by the type of loan, how long the account has been open, loan balance, and the number of late payments. The type of loan such as a mortgage with one late payment may have the same impact as three late payments on a credit card account. A newly opened loan has a greater negative impact on scores than a loan that is five years old. There should be no late payments.

Strategies Refer to #32, 40, 48, 54, 55, 57, 79, & 80.

Classic Model **3** Equifax Experian	There is usually no open revolving accounts in the credit file such as a credit card, personal line of credit, or home equity loan with a banking institution or national credit card company.

Equifax   *Too few bank revolving accounts.*
Experian   *Too few bank revolving accounts.*

Explanation   Banks and national credit card companies are considered highly valued lenders in the credit scoring system. When we do not have an open revolving account with one of these lending institutions, we fail to demonstrate that we can meet their higher loan qualifications. This factor impacts credit scores when we fail to have at least one revolving account with one of them. We don't need to have a loan balance; rather, we must simply have it open. Revolving accounts can be a credit card, home equity loan, or personal line of credit. Banks can be either federal or state chartered banks. National credit card companies include *Capital One, Discover, American Express* or other nationwide credit card lenders. Credit unions and savings and loans are not considered banks in the credit scoring system.

Strategies   Refer to #12, 15, & 18.

Classic Model **3** Trans Union	The balances on installment loans such as mortgage, auto, personal or other installment loans are excessively high and have not been paid down from their initial loan amounts.

Trans Union   *Proportion of balances to loan limits is too high.*
Equifax   *Please see code number 33 for Equifax.*
Experian   *Please see code number 33 for Experian.*

Explanation   The issue is raised when we have high loan balance ratios on installment loans. The principal loan balances are high in relation to the initial loan amounts on these loans. Since the initial loan balance on every installment loan is 100% of the initial loan amount, the scoring system provides some leniency. One installment loan generally does not raise a concern. If multiple installment loan balances are close to their initial loan limits, this can raise our level of credit risk. Both the number of installment loans and the loan balances in relation to the initial loan amounts determine this issue's impact on scores. This factor is determined from all the open installment loans and ***not all*** the open revolving and installment loans.

Strategies   Refer to #27, 28, 29, & 40.

171

Classic Model 4
Equifax
Experian

There are too many revolving accounts open with banking institutions or national credit card companies. These revolving accounts may not have balances, but still pose a risk by the sheer number of accounts open.

Equifax   *Too many bank or national revolving accounts.*
Experian   *Too many bank or national revolving accounts.*

Explanation This risk is created for our credit score when we have multiple open revolving accounts with banks or national credit card companies. It is the potential threat of having too many personal lines of credit open. Such revolving accounts include home equity loans, personal lines of credit, and credit cards. These accounts do not need balances to impact scores. These revolving accounts simply need to be open to negatively affect credit scores. Quite often, we may have multiple revolving accounts from which we have rotated some balances to lower interest rate offers and the older credit card accounts remain open.

Strategies Refer to #35.

Classic Model 4
Trans Union

There is no recent installment loan activity in the credit file primarily in the last twelve months. The credit file lacks installment loan payment activity from a mortgage, education, auto, or personal loan.

Trans Union — *Lack of recent installment loan information.*

Equifax   *Please see code number 32 for Equifax.*
Experian   *Please see code number 32 for Experian.*

Explanation Loan types continually factor into our credit score. The system requires us to have one active installment loan. We demonstrate an ongoing ability to make monthly payments when we have an open installment loan over months, years, and decades. With this issue, there are no active installment loans in the last six to twelve months in our credit file. This risk factor usually appears when the only loan activity in our credit file comes from revolving lines of credit such as a credit cards or other lines of credit. Without an active installment loan, we raise our level of risk because the system cannot give a complete judgment of our credit profile.

Strategies Refer to #13.

Classic Model **5**	There is an excessive number of loans with balances in a credit file. The total number of loans with balances from all loan types as reflected on the credit report is excessively high and poses a risk.

Equifax   *Too many accounts with balances.*
Experian   *Number of accounts with balances.*
Trans Union *Too many accounts with balances.*

Explanation One of the more common issues that substantially impacts our credit scores. A credit file shows an excessive number of loans with balances. Past a certain point, the sheer number of loans with balances is excessive and we show a lack of credit responsibility. Even though some balances may be small (as little as $1), the number of accounts with balances is high and poses a credit risk. Such accounts can be mortgages, home equity loans, education loans, auto loans, credit card, personal lines of credit and even outstanding collections. The higher number of accounts with balances, the greater negative impact on our credit score. This issue raises our risk much more than the number of accounts open because we have active debt.

Strategies Refer to #37, 43, & 46.

Classic Model **6**	A credit file has at least one past or present loan with a finance company. Having a loan with this lower valued lender poses a credit risk by identifying one we use for our financing.

Equifax   *Too many consumer finance accounts.*
Experian   *Number of finance company accounts.*
Trans Union *Too many consumer finance accounts.*

Explanation Many are unfamiliar with the different types of lenders that offer credit. This concern appears when we have at least one loan with a finance company. A finance company is high risk that usually lends to those with a lower credit rating and they can have a considerable impact on scores. Where banks are highly valued, finance companies are considered lower, less-valued lenders with credit scores. We can have one active account, or paid off the loan for years and still impact our scores. Finance companies are not banks and thus most borrow and lend money at higher interest rates. To confuse matters, many major banks even own a finance company. They finance major purchases, autos, and even some mortgage loans.

Strategies Refer to #12, 17, 38, 78, 79, & 82.

Classic Model

7

There is limited recent payment activity in the credit file. This issue impacts scores by failing to have depth in the credit file. Can appear when there is a new credit file establishing its initial credit references.

Equifax   *Account payment history is too new to rate.*
Experian   *Account payment history is too new to rate.*
Trans Union *Account payment history is too new to rate.*

Explanation One of the less common factors in the credit scoring system. This issue can be a factor with credit scores when there is a lack of payment history in the file. We may have been unable to establish any real payment history for an extended period of time in the credit file especially with a new credit file. As we open and establish payment history at least a couple of accounts, we can diminish the negative impact from this issue on our score.

Strategies Refer to #17.

Classic Model

8

A credit file shows at least one (usually multiple) inquiries in the last 12 months. The number of inquiries poses a risk as it is the first sign to the credit scoring system that we are applying for additional credit.

Equifax   *Too many inquiries in the last 12 months.*
Experian   *Number of recent inquiries.*
Trans Union *Too many inquiries in the last 12 months.*

Explanation An inquiry is simply a request by a company to review our credit report. Some inquiries impact our scores while others do not. The inquiry that actually impacts our scores is called a hard inquiry. Such inquiries usually occur when we are applying for new credit. Hard inquiries can come from a lender for a personal loan, mortgage, credit card, or other type of financing. The greater number of hard inquiries in the last twelve months, the greater the negative impact on our scores. Even one inquiry at an 800 level credit score usually shows up as a top factor impacting our scores.

Strategies Refer to #2, 3, 4, & 5.

Classic Model **9**	There is at least one recently opened loan (in the last 12 months) as reflected by the opening date on the account. Any new debt raises questions of credit responsibility and this issue just reflects that concern.

Equifax   *Too many accounts recently opened.*

Experian   *Number of accounts opened within the last 12 months.*

Trans Union   *Too many accounts recently opened.*

Explanation This factor impacts our scores from opening at least one new loan in the last 12 months. The number of new loans opened and the type of loans opened all determine this factor's impact on our scores. For example, opening three new credit cards within 12 months has a greater negative impact on scores than opening two new education loans. This factor is quite common and can have a substantial impact on our scores.

Strategies Refer to #8, 16, 33, 77, 80, & 81.

Classic Model **10**	A credit file has at least one revolving account that has a loan balance that is excessively high to the account's high credit limit. Since the balance is excessively high in relation to its limit, it creates risk to a credit score.

Equifax   *Proportion of balances to credit limits too high on revolving accounts.*

Experian   *Proportion of balances to high credit on revolving accounts.*

Trans Union   *Proportion of revolving balances to revolving credit limits is too high.*

Explanation One of the more common factors that negatively impacts a credit score. The debt ratio, or balance to high credit limit as a percentage, is excessively high on a revolving account or line of credit. This issue shows poor credit management and poses a credit risk. The greater number of accounts with the higher debt ratios determine this factor's influence on credit scores. This issue usually appears with a high balance, but can also appear when there is no high credit limit reporting on the account.

Strategies Refer to #21, 22, 23, 24, 26, 31, 45, 76, 81, & 82.

Classic Model	A credit file has at least one opened revolving loan with an excessively high balance. This issue negatively impacts scores from credit cards and personal lines of credit which have high loan balances.
11	

Equifax   *Account owed on revolving accounts is too high.*
Experian   *Amount owed on revolving accounts is too high.*
Trans Union *Amount owed on revolving accounts is too high.*

<u>Explanation</u>   Unlike the previous issue with the debt ratio, this concern arises by the amount owed on an unsecured revolving account. A credit file has at least one account balance from a credit card or personal line of credit which is excessively high. The balance, usually in the thousands of dollars, presents a credit risk by the amount owed on that account. The total amount of debt on each account and the number of unsecured revolving accounts with high balances determines the negative impact on our credit scores. This issue can have a substantial effect on our scores.

<u>Strategies</u>   Refer to #20.

Classic Model	The length of time on average all the currently active revolving accounts have been open. This issue affects scores when revolving accounts have only been open for a short period of time.
12	

Equifax   *Length of time revolving accounts have been established.*

Experian   *Length of revolving account history.*
Trans Union *Insufficient length of revolving credit history.*

<u>Explanation</u>   This issue is a more common concern with our credit scores and often appears with *"Length of time accounts have been established"* (14). Revolving accounts such as credit cards and other personal lines of credit can remain open for years and even indefinitely. We have failed on average to establish an extended payment history with our current open revolving loans. Longer, more established revolving lines of credit, carry more value for our score than those just accounts just recently opened. We demonstrate greater credit responsibility and pose less credit risk when our revolving loans have been open longer.

<u>Strategies</u>   Refer to #19.

Classic Model **13**	A recent late payment is reflected in the credit file on at least one account. The issue of how recent a late payment has occurred raises our level of risk. The more recent the late payment, the greater the impact on scores.

Equifax	*Time since delinquency is too recent or unknown.*
Experian	*Length of time (or unknown time) since account delinquent.*
Trans Union	*Time since delinquency is too recent or unknown.*

Explanation   At least one loan in the credit file has had a recent late payment and is having a negative impact on scores. The most recent late payment has usually occurred in the last 24 months and more often in the last 12 months. The recent late payment poses a credit risk because of the question whether we are able to meet our monthly debt obligations. This issues usually appears with *"Level of delinquency on accounts"* (2) and *"Serious delinquency "* (39).

Strategies   Refer to #55 & 57.

Classic Model **14**	The length of time on average for all the current open loans have been open for only a short period of time. This issue impacts our scores when we have not established a lengthy payment history with our current loans.

Equifax	*Length of time accounts have been established.*
Experian	*Length of time accounts have been established. (It was — Time since oldest trade line opened)*
Trans Union	*Insufficient length of credit history.*

Explanation   When we open a new loan, the length of payment history starts and our payment history is established over time. The longer we have a satisfactory payment history, the more value to our credit scores. Those accounts that have been open longer, with a more established payment history, carry more value with credit scores than those accounts just recently opened. We demonstrate greater credit responsibility and pose less credit risk. With this concern, all open mortgage, installment, revolving, and other accounts on average have failed to be open for an extended period of time to established a respected payment history.

Strategies   Refer to #29 & 34.

Classic Model
15
There is no recent revolving account activity with a banking institution or a national credit card company. Having at least one active revolving loan with such lenders demonstrates our ongoing credit qualification.

Equifax   *Lack of recent revolving history.*
Experian   *Lack of recent bank / national revolving information.*
Trans Union *Insufficient or lack of bank revolving account information.*

Explanation   Reason code three outlines the issue of failing to have an open revolving account with a bank or national credit card company. This issue requires us not only to have one account open, but also to periodically use at least one revolving account with a bank or national credit card company. When there is no revolving loan activity from one of these lenders, we fail to demonstrate a certain level of credit qualification. We may have even had an account with such a lender, but closed it months or years ago. Any revolving loan activity from such a qualified lender resolves this concern.

Strategies   Refer to #12, 14 & 18.

Classic Model
16
The credit file shows no open revolving account. The lack of at least one open revolving account poses a credit risk by failing to demonstrate responsibility with a proper mix of revolving and installment loans.

Equifax   *Lack of recent revolving account information.*
Experian   *Lack of recent revolving account information.*
Trans Union *Insufficient or lack of revolving account information.*

Explanation   This issue is raised when there is a lack of any revolving account activity in the file from a bank, national credit card company, or any other lender. There are no personal lines of credit, credit cards overdraft accounts or any other revolving account open in the credit file. Lenders give us a credit line that we must properly manage with revolving loans. We demonstrate greater credit responsibility and pose less credit risk when we have at least one open revolving loan. If we only have one revolving account, it should be with a bank or national credit card company (No. 3).

Strategies   Refer to #14 & 18.

Classic Model **17**	There are no accounts with loan balances in the credit file outside of a mortgage. This factor impacts scores by failing to demonstrate credit responsibility with other types of loans other than a mortgage.

Equifax   *No recent non-mortgage balance information.*
Experian   *No recent non-mortgage balance information.*
Trans Union *No recent non-mortgage balance information.*

Explanation   This is an uncommon factor with credit scores. However, there are a few instances in which the only loan balance in the credit file is the mortgage. With this issue, there is a lack of loan balances in the file from additional installment and revolving loans. A credit file lacks additional quality credit references. There is no loan balances and monthly payment history from a mixture revolving or other installment loans. Some loan activity is better than no loan activity.

Strategies   Refer to #13 & 14.

Classic Model **18**	There are at least one and usually multiple accounts in the file that have had a late payment reported. Added risk has been created by failing to maintain timely payments on all loans in the credit file.

Equifax   *Number of accounts with delinquency.*
Experian   *Number of accounts delinquent.*
Trans Union *Frequent delinquency.*

Explanation   This factor looks at the number of accounts that have been paid satisfactorily. If even one payment has been late and reported to the credit report, this account becomes delinquent for at least seven years. The number of loans delinquent can be as little as one account, or on most cases, multiple loans. This account status remains until the late payment falls from the payment history, usually at seven years. The number of loans with late payments creates added credit risk and factors into our scores.

Strategies   Refer to #50, 56, & 67.

Classic Model	The majority of accounts listed in the credit file have had at least one late payment in the payment history. A person poses a credit risk by failing to demonstrate and make timely payments on most of the loans.
19 Equifax Experian	

Equifax   *Too few accounts currently paid as agreed.*
Experian   *Too few accounts currently paid as agreed.*

Trans Union *Please see code number 27 for Trans Union.*

Explanation   The number of accounts with late payments is reported on most of the current and past accounts in the credit file. These loans include every loan reference in the file including mortgage, revolving, installment, or collection accounts. The number of accounts with late payments versus the number of total accounts is high. This factor can impact credit scores for many years until the delinquent loans have dropped from the credit file. In many cases, the issue results from having multiple collection accounts in the credit file.

Strategies   Refer to #50, 56, & 67.

Classic Model	A credit file shows an inquiry from a lender usually in the last three months. A recent inquiry can pose a credit risk as it recent in time and is the first sign that we are taking out a new loan which creates additional risk.
19 Trans Union	

Trans Union *Date of last inquiry too recent.*

Explanation   This factor is not a major issue and hardly appears at all. A recent inquiry poses a credit risk because it reveals that we are applying for a new loan in the last few months. Since the inquiry is so recent, the new loan may not appear on the credit report. This can pose a credit risk because of the uncertainty of the new loan and our ability to make timely payments on the new loan.

Strategies   Refer to #2, 3, 4, & 5.

Classic Model 20	A significant credit issue has occurred and poses a significant risk for future loan considerations. How recent and the severity of this event compound this issue's negative effect on our credit.

Equifax   *Length of time since derogatory public record or collection is too short.*

Experian   *Length of time since derogatory public record or collection is too short.*

Trans Union *Length of time since legal item filed or collection item reported.*

Explanation There are two issues; one is the length of time a serious credit issued has occurred and two, the credit issue is severe. The derogatory mark is at least one of the following: bankruptcy, judgment, federal, state or community tax lien, or a collection. This factor commonly appears with *"Derogatory public record or collection filed"* (40). Only paying off the past due amount and time can reduce this factor's influence on our credit scores.

Strategies Refer to #53, 67, 68, 70, 71, & 72.

Classic Model 21	A credit file shows at least one and usually multiple accounts that have payments or amounts currently past due. The amount past due creates a significant credit risk by revealing the amount that is currently late.

Equifax   *Amount past due on accounts.*

Experian   *Amount past due on accounts.*

Trans Union *Amount past due on accounts.*

Explanation This factor identifies past due payments on any revolving or installment loans, and collection accounts. There is a significant amount past due from the current accounts in the credit report and it has a dramatic effect on scores. The amount past due is reported in the *Past due* column of the credit report. The amount past due creates additional credit risk since we are already behind on payments, and it is undetermined whether we can continue to make timely payments going forward on all of our outstanding loans with such a substantial amount past due. This factor commonly appears with *"Level of delinquency on accounts"* (2) and *"Serious delinquency"* (39).

Strategies Refer to #47.

Classic Model	
22	No current reference with the *Classic* score model.

Equifax   *No current reference.*
Experian   *No current reference.*
Trans Union   *No current reference.*

Classic Model 23 Equifax Experian	The number of revolving accounts with balances from a banking institution or a national credit card company is excessively high. This issue creates risk by the number of accounts with balances from these type of accounts.

Equifax   *Number of bank or national revolving accounts with balances.*

Experian   *Number of bank or national revolving accounts with balances.*

Explanation   There are an excessive number of revolving accounts with balances from banks and national credit card companies. The revolving accounts can be in the form of credit cards, home equity loans, overdraft accounts, or other lines of credit. These types of accounts are not affiliated with any particular transaction. Instead, they are usually used for multiple purchases and are used to create additional debt. The number of accounts with balances creates added risk by the total number of loans with balances. This issue can become a considerable risk for credit scores.

Strategies   Refer to #25.

Classic Model

24

We may have open revolving accounts, however, there are no revolving accounts in the credit file with balances. With no recent revolving loan activity, we fail to demonstrate a certain responsibility to manage credit.

Equifax   *No recent revolving balances.*
Experian   *Lack of recent reported balances on revolving / open accounts.*
Trans Union *No recent revolving balances.*

Explanation   Reason code 15 outlines the need to have at least one open revolving account. This concern usually appears when there is no recent revolving loan activity from any of the revolving accounts including a credit card or other personal line of credit. Since there is no borrowing activity, we limit our ability to demonstrate good credit management which raises our credit risk. The amount borrowed is irrelevant and can be from any type of lender as long as the loan type is a revolving account. If we only have one account we use, it should be from a bank or national credit card company.

Strategies   Refer to #15 & 18.

Classic Model

25

No current reference with the *Classic* score model.

Equifax   *No current reference.*
Experian   *No current reference.*
Trans Union *No current reference.*

Classic Model

26

No current reference with the *Classic* score model.

Equifax   *No current reference.*
Experian   *No current reference.*
Trans Union *No current reference.*

Classic Model

27

Trans Union

The majority of accounts listed in the credit file have had at least one late payment in the payment history. A person poses a credit risk by failing to demonstrate and make timely payments on most of the loans.

Trans Union *Too few accounts currently paid as agreed.*

Equifax   *Please see code number 19 for Equifax.*
Experian   *Please see code number 19 for Experian.*

Explanation Considered a Level III delinquency. This issue impacts scores by a lack of timely payments on most of the current and past accounts in the credit file. These loans include every loan reference in the file including mortgage, revolving, installment, or collection accounts. The number of accounts with late payments versus the number of total accounts is high. This factor can impact credit scores for many years until the delinquent loans have dropped from the credit file. In many cases, the issue results from having multiple collection accounts in the credit file.

Strategies Refer to #50, 56, & 67.

Classic Model

28

The total number of open accounts with or without balances is excessive and poses a credit risk. These open accounts can be revolving, installment, mortgage or collections.

Equifax   *Number of established accounts.*
Experian   *Number of established accounts.*
Trans Union   *Too many accounts.*

Explanation   This issue usually appears when there is too many open loans in the credit file and can become a considerable factor with scores. An excessive number of loans currently open can create a credit risk by allowing too much available credit. An excessive number of loans open can also demonstrate a lack of credit management. Even though these opened loans may not have balances, they can still factor into our scores. Oftentimes, small older revolving credit card or merchant accounts may have been forgotten and left open, and impact our scores down the road. We should review our credit report and identify all our open accounts.

Strategies   Refer to #16, 36, & 44.

Classic Model

29

Experian
Trans Union

There are no revolving accounts in the credit file with balances from banks or national credit card company. With no recent revolving loan activity, we fail to demonstrate credit responsibility with a valuable creditor.

Experian   *No recent bank card balances.*
Trans Union   *No recent bank card balances.*

Equifax   *No current reference.*

Explanation   Reason codes three and four outline the requirement to have at least one revolving account open with a bank or national credit card company, but not too many open. Reason code 23 raises an issue when we have too many of these accounts with balances. This concern usually appears when there is no recent revolving loan activity with a bank or national credit company. We limit our ability to demonstrate ongoing debt management from a quality lender. The amount borrowed can be small as long as the loan type is a bank or national credit card revolving account.

Strategies   Refer to #12, 15, & 18.

Classic Model	The time since the last account opening is relatively recent and poses a credit risk to properly manage our credit. It poses a concern until the account becomes more established.
30	

Equifax　　*Time since recent account opening is too short.*

Experian　　*Time since most recent account opening is too short.*

Trans Union　*Time since most recent account opening is too short.*

Explanation　Any new loan creates additional risk. This factor can impact scores for several months immediately after opening a new loan. There are questions whether we can make timely payments on the new loan. Do we have the financial resources and the responsibility to make timely payments? Opening a new loan creates some of the highest credit risk. For this reason, we should limit new loans after we have an established credit file.

Strategies　Refer to #33, 77, & 80.

Classic Model	There is no payment activity made on any accounts in the credit file over the last several months. Since there is no payment activity, the system cannot measure our credit risk.
31 Equifax Experian	

Experian　　*Too few accounts with recent payment information.*

Equifax　　*Too few accounts with current payment information.*

Trans Union　*Please see code number 34 for Trans Union.*

Explanation　This issue is highly uncommon with credit scores. The credit file may have accounts open, but there is no recent payment activity. We build our credit by making timely payments on accounts. When there are no accounts with recent payments made, we fail to build our credit standing. With no recent payment activity, we can raise our level of credit risk.

Strategies　Refer to #13 & 14.

Classic Model

31

Trans Union

The outstanding balance on an account that is currently or has been recently late with monthly payments is high. The loan balance on that particular delinquent loan is high and poses a risk to a person's credit stability.

Trans Union   *Amount owed on delinquent account.*

Equifax   *Please see code number 34 for Equifax.*
Experian   *Please see code number 34 for Experian.*

Explanation   The size of any loan can pose a credit risk. Monthly payments are higher and the chance of default are greater. However, this risk increases considerably when a large loan such as a mortgage or an auto loan has had a late payment. Once an account has had a late payment, it is reflected in the credit file as a delinquent account and can impact scores for years.

Strategies   Refer to #55, 57, & 65.

Classic Model

32

Equifax Experian

There is no recent installment loan activity in the credit file primarily in the last twelve months. The credit file lacks installment loan payment activity from a mortgage, education, auto, or personal loan.

Equifax   *Lack of recent installment loan information.*
Experian   *Lack of recent installment loan information.*

Trans Union   *Please see code number 4 for Trans Union.*

Explanation   Loan types continually factor into our credit score. The system requires us to have one active installment loan. We demonstrate an ongoing ability to make monthly payments when we have an open installment loan over months, years, and decades. There are no active installment loans in the last six to twelve months in our credit file. This risk factor usually appears when the only loan activity in our credit file comes from revolving lines of credit such as a credit cards or other lines of credit. Without an active installment loan, we raise our level of risk because the system cannot give a complete judgment of our credit profile.

Strategies   Refer to #13.

Classic Model	The balances on installment loans such as mortgage, auto, personal or other installment loans are excessively high and have not been paid down from their initial loan amounts.
33	

Equifax   *Proportion of loan balances to loan limits is too high.*
Experian   *Proportion of loan balances to original loan limit.*
Trans Union   *Please see code number 3 for Trans Union.*

Explanation   The issue is raised when we have a high loan balance ratios on installment loans. The principal loan balances are high in relation to the initial loan amounts on these loans. Since the initial loan balance on every installment loan is 100% of the initial loan amount, the scoring system provides some leniency. One installment loan erases this concern. If multiple installment loan balances are close to their initial loan limits, this can raise our level of credit risk. Both the number of installment loans and the loan balances in relation to the initial loan amounts determine this issue's impact on scores. Unlike factor 1, this factor is determined from all the open installment loans and ***not all*** the open revolving and installment loans.

Strategies   Refer to #27, 28, 29, & 40.

Classic Model	The outstanding balance on an account that is currently or has been recently late with monthly payments is high. The loan balance on that particular delinquent loan is high and poses a risk to a person's credit stability.
34 Equifax Experian	

Experian   *Amount owed on delinquent account.*
Equifax   *Amount owed on delinquent account.*

Trans Union   *Please see code number 31 for Trans Union.*

Explanation   The size of any loan can pose a credit risk. Monthly payments are higher and the chance of default is greater. However, this risk increases considerably when a large loan such as a mortgage or an auto loan has had a late payment. Once an account has had a late payment, it is reflected in the credit file as a delinquent account and can impact scores for years.

Strategies   Refer to #55, 57, & 65.

Classic Model

35

No current reference with the *Classic* score model.

Equifax   *No current reference.*
Experian   *No current reference.*
Trans Union *No current reference.*

Classic Model

36

No current reference with the *Classic* score model.

Equifax   *No current reference.*
Experian   *No current reference.*
Trans Union *No current reference.*

| Classic Model **37** | No current reference with the *Classic* score model. |

Equifax   *No current reference.*
Experian   *No current reference.*
Trans Union *No current reference.*

| Classic Model **38** | A credit file has an account that had at least one loan with multiple late payments after a bankruptcy, judgment, tax lien, or collection. The seriousness of both issues can affect scores for several years. |

Experian   *Serious delinquency and derogatory public record or collection filed..*

Equifax   *Serious delinquency, and public record or collection filed.*

Trans Union *Serious delinquency, and public record or collection filed.*

Explanation   Considered a Level IV delinquency or continual delinquency. Commonly referred as the 'Black hole', this factor has the greatest negative impact on credit scores for years. This issue appears when we have had consecutive late payments on at least one loan after a bankruptcy, judgment, tax lien, or collection. We show poor credit responsibility from the prior public record or collection, and a second time later from the additional late payments.

Strategies   Refer to #53, 64, 67, 69, 70, 71, & 72.

Classic Model

39

At least one current or past loan in the credit file shows multiple late payments at one time or a series of late payments over a period of time. One loan has fallen seriously past due in its payments.

Equifax   *Serous delinquency.*
Experian   *Serious delinquency.*
Trans Union *Serious delinquency.*

Explanation   There is a certain threshold that if we pass, the level of delinquency is serious and has an influence on our scores for years. The account that triggered this factor can even be paid off and still impact our scores. When an account has at least two consecutive late payments or its payments are at least two payments delinquent, we are considered, 'Seriously delinquent.' This factor has one of the greatest negative impacts on scores.

Strategies   Refer to #40, 61, & 73.

Classic Model

40

A credit file shows a bankruptcy, tax lien, judgment in the public record section, or a collection in the payment history section. This level of delinquency is severe and negatively impact credit scores for several years.

Experian   *Derogatory public record or collection filed.*
Equifax   *Derogatory public record or collection filed.*
Trans Union *Derogatory public record or collection filed.*

Explanation   A credit file shows a bankruptcy, tax lien, judgment in the public record's section, or a collection in the account history section of the credit report. The judgment, tax lien, or collection can be paid and still impact credit scores for up to ten years. An unpaid tax lien can be indefinite. A bankruptcy appears when we file a Chapter 7 or Chapter 13 bankruptcy. A judgment shows when a court of law has found a civil judgment or a fine been issued. A tax lien comes from a local, state, or federal past tax that is unpaid. A collection appears from a collection agency when an account is usually six months or more past due.

Strategies   Refer to #53, 63, 64, 67, 69, 70, 71, & 72.

Bibliography

Better Business Bureau Online. *New Research Shows Identity Fraud Growth is Contained and Consumers Have More Control than They Think.* January 31, 2006. www.bbbonline.org/idtheft/safetyquiz.asp.

Cassady, Allison. National Association of State PIRGs. *Mistakes Do Happen: A Look at Errors in Consumer Credit Reports.* June 2004. http://www.masspirg.org/reports/MistakesDoHappen2004MA. Pages 4-16.

MyFICO, a division of Fair Isaac Corporation. *Understanding Your FICO Score.* http://www.ucu.maine.edu/understandingcreditscore 1-17.

Federal Trade Commission. *FTC Releases Survey of Identity Theft in U.S. 27.3 Million Victims in Past 5 Years, Billions of Losses for Businesses and Consumers.* Released September 3, 2003.

Federal Trade Commission. *FTC Sues "Credit Repair" Companies.* Released January 27, 2005.

Fedderman, Mindy, and Barbara Hansen. *Young People Struggle to Deal with the Kiss of Debt.* (USA Today, November 20, 2006) 1A-2A. Experian completed an analysis for USA Today from credit records of twenty-somethings from August 1, 2001 to August 1, 2006.

Interview with an insurance agent. June 6, 2006. (Research found on page 3) All interviews were conducted in confidentiality and the name of the interviewee is withheld by mutual agreement.

MyFICO's official website (MyFICO is a division of Fair Isaac Corporation), http://www.myfico.com. Average interest rates. June 6, 2006.

Webster's New World Dictionary and Thesaurus, 2nd ed. (Wiley Publishing Inc., 2002), 331.

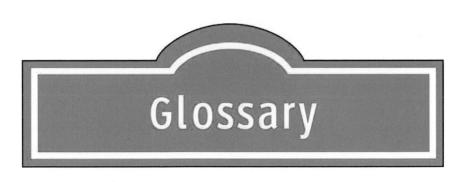

Glossary

Account: The lender of record in the credit file.

Account History: Also known as payment history. Most credit reports show a monthly payment history for the last 24 months on a month-by-month basis. Any late payments will show for seven years under the account history.

Account Status: Shows the current account status and any delinquencies or late payments.

Account Closed: A loan reported to the credit bureaus as closed or no longer open and inaccessible for additional credit.

Active Account: An open loan that may or may not have a loan balance.

Address: The current and former addresses are displayed in the personal information section of the credit report. The most recent address known to the credit bureaus is reported as the current address. Any creditor reporting an incorrect address to the credit bureaus different than the current address may change the permanent address in the credit file.

Amount Past Due: The amount on a loan as shown on a credit report that is currently past due.

Authorized User Account: A revolving loan that has added a person to the loan by permission of the initial borrower and the creditor.

Balance: Amount owed on a loan at the time the information was updated from the lender to the credit bureau on the last reporting date.

Bankruptcy: A public record when a person has sought financial relief from his creditors through court filing to relieve a person's debt payments. Bankruptcy can occur as a chapter 11 with repayment options, or a chapter 7 with total liquidation of debts.

Birthday: The date of record in the credit file showing the birthday which is one means to identify an individual.

Closed Account: A loan that is no longer open. A closed loan can be paid off or is no longer open to additional credit requests.

Collection: An account which has gone to a collection agency who specializes in collecting past due debts.

Cosigner: A person who signs with another individual to qualify for a loan.

Credit File: A collection of personal information, account and payment information, and public records created and organized by each credit bureaus. A credit file is created for each individual by the credit bureaus to track account and payment history on those accounts which report to the credit bureau. The credit bureaus identify and authenticate the information coming in from various sources and designate that information to a credit file. The credit report is simply a compilation of all the information gathered in that credit file.

Credit Limit: The total line of credit or high credit limit available on a revolving account. This amount is critical in determining the debt ratio.

Credit Report: The information compiled and communicated by the credit bureaus from a person's past credit history to an outside party. The report shows most of the information contained in a credit file. Names and variation of a person's name, addresses, public records, account information, and inquiries. Credit scores may or may not be a part of the credit report.

Credit Risk Factor: Also called reason codes. They are the risk factors that negatively impact credit scores. The top four or five reasons are usually provided by the credit bureaus when a credit score is given.

Credit Score: A three-digit number provided by each credit bureau to determine a our credit risk. This credit score can be calculated from one of three models; *Classic, NextGen,* and *Vantage.* The three models also have slight scoring variations of each model which can give a minor modification of a credit score.

Credit Summary: A compiled list of loans broken down into credit limits, balances, types of loans, monthly payments, and any delinquent payments found in the credit file. It also includes the oldest credit reference, the worst credit rating, and the number of inquiries found in the credit report.

Creditor: A lender of record in the credit file. Lenders can show under different names or symbols in the credit file.

Date on File: The date the credit bureau opened a credit file on a person.

Debt: The amount owed on all current outstanding loans.

Debt-to-High Credit Limit Ratio (Debt Ratio): The ratio calculated by dividing the outstanding balance into the high credit limit on a revolving account. A revolving account can be a credit card, personal line of credit, overdraft account, or a home equity loan. This ratio helps determine if we have mismanaged our debt by being over-extended.

Delinquent Account: A loan in the credit file that has had at least one late payment in its payment history over the last seven years.

Dispute Letter: A letter sent to the credit bureaus to ask that particular information be corrected on a credit file.

Employer: The employer of record in the credit file meant to identify current and past employers of an individual. It is one of the means used by credit bureaus to identify a person's information.

Equifax: One of the three major credit bureaus that compiles a credit file and distributes its information to companies nationwide.

Experian: One of the three major credit bureaus that compiles a credit file and distributes its information to companies nationwide.

Filing Date: The month and year the public record was filed with the courts.

High Credit Limit or Initial Loan Balance: It is the credit limit established by a lender for the amount we can borrow on a revolving account. It is also the initial loan or highest balance since the loan was opened on an installment loan.

Identification: The personal information of name, social security number, birthday, and address of the person on record in the credit file.

Inquiry: A request for a person's credit report from a company. The list of inquiries showing each company the date of the credit report request is shown for the past 24 months in the Inquiry section of the credit report.

Judgment: A public record from a civil or criminal case when a civil amount was levied against a person. The creditor then has additional options to collect the amount awarded by the court. Stays on a credit report for up to seven years.

Last Active Date (also called Status Date): The month and year when the loan last had any payment or loan activity. Seven years from the last active date is the time when the account will drop from the credit file and no longer be displayed in the report.

Lenders:

> **Auto:** Lenders that specialize in financing autos.

> **Banking Institutions:** A lender that take deposits and establish checking and saving accounts. Credit unions along with banks are considered banking institutions under the credit scoring model.

> **Finance Company:** Privately funded companies that finance loans. They are considered higher risk lenders in the credit score models with higher interest rates and fees.

> **Mortgage Company:** Lenders that specialize in real estate loans.

> **National Credit Card Company**: National lenders that primarily offer credit card services to consumers throughout the country.

> **Payday Lender:** Privately funded companies that finance smaller personal loans. They are also considerably higher risk in the credit score models with higher interest rates and fees.

> **Retail or Merchant Lender:** Lenders that specialize in financing the purchases of their clientele.

Loan Type: The type of loan as reflected on the credit report. A loan can be a mortgage, installment, or revolving.

Loan Balance Ratio: The ratio calculated by dividing the outstanding loan balance into the initial loan amount on an installment loan. An installment loan can be a mortgage, auto, education, or personal loan. This ratio determines how much we have paid down our loan from the initial loan amount.

Loans:

> **Closed:** A loan that has been closed and cannot be used for additional credit.

> **Duplicate:** A loan which appears twice on the same credit bureau file.

> **Installment:** A loan with consistent monthly payments made over a set period of time until the loan is either paid off or refinanced.

Mortgage: A loan secured by a home or real estate.

New: A loan recently opened in the last 12 months.

Open: An active loan that may or may not have a balance.

Revolving: Payments made on the outstanding balance of the loan. The payments can vary depending on what the balance is. The term of the loan can be set or be indefinite.

Secured: A loan which is secured with some type of asset such as an auto, home, or other personal items.

Unsecured: An established loan that has no security attached to the loan. If the loan goes into default, the lender cannot repossess the property.

Open Date: The month and year an account whether currently active or inactive was opened.

Payment History: The payment history in the credit report from each loan that reflects on-time payments, or payments that have been late in the last seven years. The late payments can reflect a 30, 60, 90, 120, 150, or 180 days late. The payment history is the highest contributing factor to the credit scoring system.

Payments:

Late: Payments that are late on an account. Such payments can be 30 days or more late and will reflect as delinquent or derogatory mark on the account.

Timely: Monthly payments that are made on time and show no history of late payments over 30 days..

30 Day Late: A late payment that was at least 30 days or one payment past due.

60 Day Late: A loan payment that was at least 60 days or two payments past due.

90 Day Late: A loan payment that was at least 90 days or three payments past due.

120 Day Late: A loan payment that was at least 120 days or four payments past due.

150 Day Late: A loan payment that was at least 150 days or five payments past due.

180 Day Late: A loan payment that was at least 180 days or six payments past due.

Personal Information: The information gathered by the credit bureaus for each credit file that identifies a person's name, social security number, birth date, current and former addresses, and employment.

Public Record: A section in the credit report which identifies any public records. This public record include any bankruptcies, judgments, and tax liens as provided by the a court.

Reason Codes: The top factors listed with each credit score. These codes highlight those factors that most negatively influencing the credit scores at a particular time. They are also called credit risk factors.

Reporting Date: The most recent month and year a lender has reported account information to a credit file.

Social Security Number: The nine digit number given to each legal citizen or authorized worker in the United States. The principal driver of the credit files. Credit files are compiled primarily through the social security number.

Tax Lien: A past due amount established by a federal, state or local government agency that has not been paid in a timely manner.

Trade Line: An account found in the credit file and displayed in a credit report. A trade line identifies the lender, the opening date, last active date, reporting date, high credit limit, loan balance, past due amount, type of account, and payment history.

Trans Union: One of the three major credit bureaus that compiles a credit file and distributes its information to companies nationwide.

Index

A

B

C

G

H

I

J

L

M

N

O

P

R

S

T

U

V